Measuring the Value of the Supply Chain

Measuring the Value of the Supply Chain

Linking Financial Performance and Supply Chain Decisions

ENRICO CAMERINELLI

GOWER

Published by
Gower Publishing Limited
Wey Court East
Union Road
Farnham
Surrey, GU9 7PT
England

Ashgate Publishing Company
Suite 420
101 Cherry Street
Burlington,
VT 05401-4405
USA

www.gowerpublishing.com

British Library Cataloguing in Publication Data
Camerinelli, Enrico
   Measuring the value of supply chain : linking financial
   performance and supply chain decisions
   1. Business logistics
   I. Title
   658.5

   ISBN: 978-0-566-08794-3

Library of Congress Control Number: 2008932659

Mixed Sources
Product group from well-managed
forests and other controlled sources
www.fsc.org Cert no. SA-COC-1565
© 1996 Forest Stewardship Council
FSC

Printed and bound in Great Britain by
MPG Books Ltd, Bodmin, Cornwall.

Contents

List of Figures

List of Tables

List of Abbreviations

APQC	American Productivity and Quality Center
ATM	automated teller machine
ATP	available-to-promise
BOM	bill of materials
BVA	business value added
CAPS	Centre for Advanced Purchasing Studies
CFO	chief financial officer
COGS	cost of goods sold
CRM	customer relationship management
C2C	cash-to cash cycle time
DIO	days inventory outstanding
DPO	days purchasing outstanding
DSO	days sales outstanding
EBIT	earnings before income taxes
EIPP	electronic invoice presentation and payment
ERP	Enterprise Resource Planning
ETO	engineer-to-order

EVA   economic value added

FMCG   fast-moving consumer goods

FTL   full-truckload

GAAP   generally accepted accounting principles

GRN   goods receipt note

IFRS   International Financial Reporting Standards

IT   information technology

JPM   J.P. Morgan Chase

LC   letter of credit

LTL   less-than-truckload

MRP   Materials Requirements Planning

MTO   make-to-order

MTS   make-to-stock

NAICS   North American Industry Classification

NOPAT   net operating profit after taxes

OGC   Office of Government Commerce

OTIF   on-time-in-full

POD   proof of delivery

PP&E   property, plant and equipment

PRTM   Pittiglio Rabin Todd & McGrath

ROIC   return on invested capital

S&OP   sales and operations planning

SCOR™   Supply Chain Operations Reference™

SEPA   Single Euro Payments Area

SG&A   selling, general and administrative expenses

SIC   Standard Industry Classification

SCC   Supply Chain Council

TRS   total return to shareholders

TSU   Trade Services Utility

WACC   weighted average cost of capital

Preface

The latest new economic scenarios for buyers and suppliers, the introduction of the Euro, the need for competition based on quality of products and company organization and the request for new services and solutions to face the new challenges of the world-wide market, has made financial institutions reconsider and remodel their approach to customers.

The complexity of customers' needs is constantly growing. This is due to technical and legal innovation, automation of administrative and financial activities, the development of networks and document dematerialization as well as reorganization of processes and relations with counterparts, all of which generate real transformations.

Nowadays sourcing managers are committed to making production workflows as smooth as possible and reducing the verticalization of production. Since supply sources are more and more global, the producers perform less and less the full production cycle in-house, choosing to exploit the advantages of outsourcing instead. As a consequence up to 75 per cent of production costs, which corresponds to 55 per cent of turnover, is generated by suppliers.

What is the impact of this trend on financial flows? How can the need of suppliers to have more rapid payments and that of buyers to extend deferred payments be combined?

The production chain, based on a global and diversified supply line, allows a higher elasticity of production costs in the meantime and reduces the control on financial costs charged by suppliers. In fact, they often have to bear the weight generated by both financing their working capital during production and the liquidity gap between shipment and payment.

If we consider that supplier credit is one of the main financial sources but also the most expensive, the need to improve this area of business becomes evident and the bank can be a valid partner. The buyer makes a lot of effort to decrease costs in the internal production phase. Unfortunately, the financial supply chain has not changed much in the last 40 years: further added value can therefore be bought by accurate financial management, offering appropriate solutions, increasing payment flows and providing new services to reduce operative costs.

Along the production and supply chain different events can harm cash flows and delay payments. While the standard financing tools, typical of the banking business, are well known, the same cannot be said for the services that banks offer to companies in the different phases of the supply chain: shipping insurance, commercial information on trade partners, Purchase Order Presentment and Payment, Purchase Order Matching, Electronic Invoices Presentment and Electronic Invoices Archiving, along with tools that help suppliers to optimize their internal process flows such as letters of credit.

UniCredit Group, for example, has invested human and financial resources to develop this area of business, leveraging on its IT and technology skills to serve the new needs of corporate customers. Through Global Transaction Banking, the product factory for international transaction banking, UniCredit Group serves its clients' businesses across 22 countries in continental Europe – the core of an international network that spans more than 50 countries – with distinguished products, services and cutting-edge solutions in the areas of cash management and e-banking, structured trade and export finance, international and correspondent banking and trade finance. As a result, UniCredit is able to meet its corporate clients' transaction banking needs with a deeply rooted market presence and the capability to understand local needs and match them with best of breed technological solutions.

A financial institution's aim, when approaching companies as a Supply Chain Management partner, is to have a new mind-set, paying attention to different needs, trying to understand the dynamics of the productive world and aiming at becoming a long term business consulting partner, sharing knowledge, language and goals with its customers. Modern banks are in fact fully part of the supply chain and share with their customers the same interest in smoothness and soundness of the entire process and in the financial strength of all parties in order to guarantee business sustainability in time. The main goal for financial institutions, in this new world of ever changing dynamics, is to optimize their customers' working capital, liaising not only with Treasury or Finance Departments but also with the Sourcing Department, providing the latter with additional negotiation tools for both internal and external customers.

As an international bank, we at UniCredit have therefore enthusiastically and thankfully welcomed this opportunity to give our view on this subject. The aim is that this area of mutual interest, well developed in this book, leads to further innovation of business models and financial products and services.

Marco Bolgiani
Head of Global Transaction Banking Division, UniCredit Group.

Introduction

The rise to prominence of supply chain management in recent years has gone hand-in-hand with significant improvements in both process efficiency and the capability of supply chain technology. As this progress continues some important questions are raised for supply chain professionals – how to position their role within a business, embed it properly and give it the prominence and strategic consideration that it now deserves.

Much has already been written about how to drive efficiency in the supply chain through improving technology and processes. In this book I want to look beyond those factors to examine the implications of supply chain management for the other parts of a business. Ultimately, I want to provide insight that will give senior executives enough faith to believe that supply chain management delivers as much value as sales and marketing.

There is now a greater understanding of supply chain management than ever before, so I do not intend to explore in great detail what is already a familiar concept, but will instead look briefly at how supply chain management arrived at where it is today. Nor do I intend to recommend what I believe are the most effective market practices, nor what technology and optimization solutions a company should put in place. Similarly, I do not wish to dwell on the effects of globalization or other trends currently shaping the demands made of the supply chain, except to help define the environment in which today's supply chain managers must operate. There is already an abundance of material on these subjects, some of which I will draw upon to support the conclusions I will make throughout this book, just as I will examine some specific examples of how the supply chain can be managed in ways that deliver efficiency and noticeable performance improvement.

Primarily, I will use the following chapters to show how current views of the supply chain are challenged in a rapidly evolving marketplace and to look in more detail at:

- how evolution in the market has affected the supply chain manager's role

- how supply chain management should be viewed as a corporate asset

- how financial services organizations play a crucial role in the supply chain

- how the role of the CFO is changing

- how the value of the supply chain can be better monitored and evaluated

- how to improve communication between operations and the finance function

- how the supply chain manager impacts on the organization's overall performance.

My main aim is to investigate the impact that supply chain management and operations can have on other aspects of an organization, which elements should be considered most important for a business, and how they can play a vital role in improving overall performance.

Supply chain management can help an organization achieve many important goals, not least of which is the ability to balance demand from the market with available supply. At present, it is not necessarily clear to many organizations how all the constituent parts of supply chain management fit with the other parts of their business, nor how its components interact. I aim to shed light on these matters in the following pages and, as a consequence, I hope to show that, by realizing the true value of supply chain management, a business can achieve greater competitive differentiation in the marketplace.

Enrico Camerinelli

PART I

Current Thinking on Supply Chain Measurement

1

Supply Chain Management Today

The supply chain is playing an increasingly important part in defining companies' competitive positioning and, ultimately, their success in the marketplace. Consequently, in most organizations, the role of supply chain management is growing rapidly, as is awareness of this role. However, many companies remain unclear about precisely how to define supply chain management or how to integrate it with those parts of their business that are conventionally associated with the generation of revenue. This lack of clarity means that, understandably, organizations find it difficult to optimize their supply chains in response to the rapidly changing dynamics of today's markets.

The questions that senior managers are asking themselves about supply chain management not only indicate their strong desire to close this gap in understanding, but also highlight shortcomings in the methods they currently use to analyze their supply chains.

Typically, they want to know:

- What do supply chains look like?

- Which elements of each supply chain should my company *own* rather than have supplied as a service by another company?

- What are the typical cycle times for each stage of our supply chain?

- What are the typical cash cycles associated with our supply chain?

To begin to answer some of these questions and show that organizations need to adopt a more sophisticated approach to supply chain analysis I will look at how what we now describe as supply chain management has come into being. In doing so I will show how the trends that have shaped it in the past are still playing out today. In today's successful enterprises the greater emphasis placed on supply chain management is not only changing the approach towards the familiar processes of forecasting and sales and operations planning (S&OP), but is also redefining the concept of visibility to deliver more detailed insight into how best to bring products and services to market. We will also see that technology will play a key role in defining the future of supply chain management.

A Brief History of Supply Chain Management

Managerial attitudes towards defining supply chain management have always been highly dependent on market conditions and the imperatives that drive their organizations' strategic goals. The same is true in today's increasingly dynamic markets.

The integration of logistics processes, which ultimately gave birth to what we now term supply chain management, is nothing new, as observed by Dr Donald Bowersox, University Professor and Dean Emeritus at Michigan State University, who describes it as the third stage of evolution in a process that started in the 1960s when – despite the emergence of physical distribution management in the 1950s – there was a highly fragmented approach to logistics.[1] At that time companies began to realize that changing their organizational structure could reveal opportunities to reduce distribution costs. This led to managers increasingly becoming responsible for inventory control, and, from this point on, approaches to physical distribution matured quickly, with an emphasis on customer service changing the demands on logistics management. A greater understanding of how logistics affects cash flow encouraged efforts to integrate distribution with materials management.

Integrated logistics management took off in the 1980s, with organizations bringing together inbound and outbound processes. Although they were driven primarily by the desire to reduce costs, their efforts also gave rise to the concept of the value chain as a tool for enabling the kind of strategic planning that could deliver competitive advantage. Following the logical course of evolution of logistics management, supply chain management, as it is known today, then developed in the 1990s when organizations began to look at end-to-end

---

1   D. Bowersox, 'The Logistics of the Last Quarter of the 20th Century', *Journal of Business Logistics*, 1(1), pp. 1–17.

processes, trying to break down the internal barriers, in order to create what has become known as the extended enterprise.

At its most basic, the supply chain is viewed simply as the process by which products or services are brought to market. A useful description of supply chain management comes from Martin Christopher, Professor of Marketing and Logistics at the Cranfield School of Management, who defines it as follows:

> Supply chain management encompasses both the internal management of the logistics processes that supports the flow of product and related information, as well as the upstream and downstream linkages with suppliers and customers.[2]

Viewed within this broad definition, the supply chain can take many forms depending on the structure of a business, the nature of the industry in which it operates and its strategic goals. Many organizations can be links in this chain – raw materials suppliers, contract manufacturers, third-party logistics providers, or transportation and warehousing companies, to name but a few. This broadening of the context in which companies view their supply chains can help them recognize how they interact with other business processes and, therefore, how they can add more value than is currently perceived.

Market conditions are far more dynamic now than at any time in the past. Looking at supply chain management in a wider context – one that takes into account the manner in which markets are evolving – will certainly help supply chain managers answer their questions about their supply chains, but may also help them better articulate the very questions they ask.

The Supply Chain Perspective on Forecasting

For most companies, forecasting – the analysis of current and historical data to determine future market trends – is a familiar activity that remains extremely important in enabling them to achieve their strategic goals. It is generally applied to demand patterns in order to define customers' potential future behaviour and has become a prominent focal point for most enterprises, as they need to know well in advance the likely demand profiles they will face. In developing their forecasting techniques companies have worked to shorten the time horizon as far as possible so that they can make earlier and more

---

2   Interview with Professor Martin Christopher.

accurate predictions, thereby giving themselves more room for manoeuvre when preparing and planning their business strategies.

From a supply chain management perspective, however, it has become clear that forecasting should not focus solely on predicting demand as it has often done in the past. Instead, enterprises need to apply more accurate forecasting techniques to their supply response. In this way they will be able to position themselves better to cope with the increasingly complex, dynamic and global markets in which they must operate.

Current and historical data analysis should inform supplier management, production operations, logistics, transportation and returns management. At present it is generally assumed that customer demand forecasts are the only information needed and that data on sales volumes can be broken down into predicted volumes for the other domains through correlation tables. Such an assumption holds true in stable environments where demand can be modelled using stochastic modelling techniques based on cause-and-effect correlations. In reality, however, the current business world is far more unpredictable than such methods allow for and cannot be easily framed within a stable model.

Some argue that unpredictability is nothing new and that it has always been a feature of any market; hence the creation of forecasting techniques in the first place. That is certainly true to an extent, but the unpredictable information that has been taken into account in the past related mainly to the quantity of goods an enterprise needed to sell. In today's more dynamic business environment there are several other unpredictable factors to take into account, namely:

- multiple product categories

- associated services

- rapidly changing consumer tastes

- price rebates due to stiff – and often unfair – competition from countries in the Far East.

Since any deviation of the actual values from those forecasted could result in a huge negative impact on company profitability, companies must address these new variables and can do so in several ways. For example, they could shift away from centralized and automatic algorithm-based planning and forecasting towards an increasingly collaborative approach. Shared knowledge about market conditions, domain expertise and common sense now provide the results that were once automatically calculated by complex, multi-level algorithms. Enterprise application software that enables collaboration, dialogue and opportunity-based decisions now often sits beside the rigid and mechanical computation modules that have traditionally been used in the past. Forecasting software is therefore a support mechanism for the human-based, collaborative decision-making process.

Sales and Operations Planning

Having recognized the new demands on forecasting, the next step is to consider how to analyze current data to develop and implement specific courses of action for future operations over a specified time period. In other words, we move from forecasting to planning, which requires that enterprises examine the entire spectrum of their supply chain processes and thereby derive its value.

There is evidence that many enterprises are already looking to move beyond simple forecasting based on algorithms towards more collaborative planning methods. Many are looking with great interest at how to develop sales and operations planning. In most cases, Sales and Operations Planning (S&OP) is performed monthly, with senior management teams balancing profitability objectives, channel requirements and the organization's overall business strategy to decide how best to balance demand with supply, using such tools as a consensus-based demand plan, a constraint-based supply plan and an agreed process to bring the two together. This approach enables them to focus on the most profitable customers or, at the very least, on serving them more effectively.

Sales and Operations Planning basically drives a profitable balance between demand and supply. It helps to provide a vital understanding of important measures, such as the actual level of customer demand, which sectors of that demand are more or less profitable, and what constraints on supply a company faces. It also emphasizes the importance of establishing a collaborative demand plan across the many departments within the organization and involves customers in the definition of this plan. Good S&OP processes have been important for many years, but the decisions that companies must make based on such planning have become significantly more complex. Customers are more demanding, the number of distribution channels has grown, demand schedules are more volatile and the business environment is more competitive. Sales and operations planning processes must adapt to these new market dynamics.

According to industry analysts, successful projects for S&OP implementation focus more on change management and process alignment than on technology, but information technology (IT) has become an essential element in coping with the ever-increasing complexity of processes and is a vital process enabler for a new approach to S&OP. Recent studies conducted by industry analysts have revealed that initiatives to enhance S&OP can, on average, result in 30 per cent improvement in order fill rates and 25 per cent higher gross margins.[3]

Clearly, predicting only one possible future is no longer sufficient. Instead, supply chain managers must plan for a range of different scenarios, and this can only be achieved by creating an environment in which the many partners in the supply chain can effectively collaborate to model different possible outcomes and align their activities to accommodate many different supply scenarios. Yet, although collaborative forecasting and planning is at the centre of a company's demand generation process, a strong strategic trend across large and medium-sized organizations is currently emerging: this aims to anticipate – rather than merely react to – market tendencies and needs, as we can see in the case of a pharmaceutical company with a keen eye on innovation.

CASE STUDY: LABORATOIRES EXPANSCIENCE

French pharmaceutical company Laboratoires Expanscience has built its international business on product innovation, rigorous management and realistic project planning. Its forecasting process has moved from a system-based to a collaborative approach involving its many supply chain partners.

The company's methodology begins with its estimated sales figures, which are compared to, and matched against, the effective volumes of past sales. The historical data are first cleaned up to remove spikes in volume generated by promotions, stock-outs and seasonal market trends and the resulting data serve as a useful basis for estimating demand generation. Then, at central group level, a system-based algorithm is applied to the data to automatically generate demand forecasts. The process then moves to the level of divisional subsidiaries, where each country manager generates a manual projection supported by a collaborative demand planning suite that is provided by the enterprise software solution. The overall forecast figures are then consolidated from the automated calculation process and the manual adjustments that might be required. Of crucial importance is the way in which the quality of the

---

3   K. O'Marah and J. Souza, 'DDSN: 21st Century Supply on Demand', AMR Research, 12 August 2004, at: http://www.amrresearch.com/Content/View.asp?pmillid=17484.

forecast is measured in order to assess the reliability of the proposed figures for the last quarter against actuals.

This collaborative process allows the company to take a proactive approach to managing the future demand and supply schedules, with planning, rather than mere forecasting, being the predominant activity.

Most pharmaceutical companies still struggle with organizational structures based on silos such as research, development, production and commercial operations. Defining – or redefining – the S&OP process is the best opportunity such companies have to break down the walls between those silos and introduce the concept of the value chain. This is what Laboratoires Expanscience has done. Like many large or medium-sized organizations, it sees the value in collaborative forecasting and planning and is becoming more proactive in anticipating demand and supply schedules to drive the innovation that is vital for its business.

Laboratoires Expanscience's strategic programme will become its main competitive tool for survival and expansion. To intercept unpredicted events, mitigate disruption and enable management to make better decisions more quickly it has identified the strategic levers in the areas of processes, organization and systems/IT applications that dramatically reduce the need to 'guesstimate' sales volumes. The company systematically measures the performance of each supply chain process and has a policy of developing win–win partnerships with customers and suppliers on inventory management by providing more visibility and more accurate forecasting. Planning and operational management are an integral part of this partnership policy. This is giving Laboratoires Expanscience more scope for innovation and, in the cosmetics sector for instance, it is now able to bring new-look products to the market much more frequently than ever before.

At the organizational level the company has implemented a 'lean office' project to optimize administrative processes and improve the flow of information, maintaining a continuous link between data on sales and production – two worlds that all too often have conflicting agendas and forecasts.

To further reduce uncertainty around missing predicted future sales volumes Laboratoires Expanscience has created a 'centre of excellence' which brings together experts in finance, IT and logistics to support the demand generation activities of the group subsidiaries.

The IT aspect of the company's programme includes the development of a decision support system that enables rapid feasibility analysis for conflicting scenarios. The results are then shared in a collaborative environment through Web meetings between the subsidiaries and their suppliers using an internally developed system. The company also has its own reporting system at group level that helps to manage growth across its many subsidiary divisions, enabling it to anticipate demand more consistently than would be possible if it relied solely on system-based forecasts.

Agent-based Technology: The New Frontier in Forecasting

As shown by the case study above, technology is a key component of any planning or forecasting process. In many organizations planners rely on rules-based software to support their decision-making process which also draws on their intrinsic knowledge and experience-based calculations. The software follows a formula for the allocation of resources based on predetermined decisions, suggesting that there is a simple process of cause and effect – that is, that the occurrence of event X leads to the probable outcome Y.

Whenever an unanticipated event arises at any stage in the order process, however, it will generate an exception. Many variables – such as quantity, deadline, stock-outs and machine failures – could give rise to exceptions when the system lacks the necessary information to make a decision based on its rules. It then falls to the planners to use their knowledge and experience to determine the best solution. To add a new scenario into a rules-based system to accommodate similar exceptions the planner must generate and program in new rules. In most cases, however, this would be a lengthy process, and, in the dynamic world of logistics, would often take too long to be of any practical benefit.

To solve this problem and create a more efficient and responsive supply chain, companies could incorporate all the elements in the network into a single system. This would allow the entire network to react as a unified whole to any new event that may arise. According to software vendors like Magenta Technology, systems to support this process of continuous planning are now readily available in the form of multi-agent technology.

In essence, multi-agent technology derives its value from its highly granular approach to the IT aspect of forecasting. It allows all the individual objects – or agents – that make up an application to interact intelligently with other objects in a wider system to the benefit of all the organizations involved in the supply chain. Each agent is subject to its own needs, constraints, attributes and preferences. Each link in the supply chain constantly communicates, negotiates and trades with the other agents, which are also seeking to maximize the benefit of their supply chain relationships and improve the performance of the overall system. Any agent can perceive events as they arise and then assess their impact, plan a response and act appropriately in a coordinated fashion. Furthermore, they will be aware of the need to request help from their supply chain partners should an event give rise to a situation they feel they cannot adequately handle on their own. Problem-solving becomes far quicker and easier when separate modules in a supply chain network interact to allow agents to cooperate and exchange information. Achieving this goal is simply not feasible if planners are merely integrating knowledge and inference mechanisms into a single software component.

Setting up such a collaborative network may seem like a laborious process, but the effort yields rewards. Collaboration between thousands of agents can occur in seconds, making them highly alert and responsive to change.

Taking the road transport sector as an example, one agent may be an individual truck looking for a load and a driver. Another agent may be a load looking for a truck, and yet another may be a driver looking for a truck and a load. The limitations of the truck, the size of the load, its required delivery time, restrictions on and preferences of the driver are all programmed into their respective agents. This provides the collaborative framework in which to quickly determine whether an ideal outcome is possible by matching all three agents.

There are certainly other technologies that can improve the performance of the supply chain, but agent-based technology at least illustrates that, in today's business environment, supply chain management requires new branches of software development and advanced solutions that go beyond the traditional capabilities of Materials Requirements Planning (MRP) and Enterprise Resource Planning (ERP) systems.

Redefining Visibility for Today's Markets

The rapid evolution of supply chain management practices becomes obvious when we look at another issue that has become a focus for supply chain managers – visibility. In recent years there has been much debate on how to define visibility, but so far it has usually been examined in a narrow context, the focus having been largely on the specific aspects of localization and the tracking of goods. In keeping with our goal of widening the scope of debate about the supply chain and its role within an enterprise we must consider much broader definitions of visibility.

In principle, supply chain visibility helps an organization better appreciate which market sectors, distribution channels and value chain configurations will yield the highest level of competitive advantage. Many of the world's largest manufacturing companies are now reacting to current competitive constraints by adapting their approaches to enterprise supply chain management technology and processes. To begin with, they have adopted a top-down supply chain management 'waterfall' process model, in which a high-level design of the supply network lays the foundation for subsequent strategic demand and tactical production planning phases, which in turn generate an execution model for processes such as manufacturing and logistics. They now plan their supply chains as a combination of component solutions that enable better visibility of both inbound and outbound processes. These components include the ability to perform the following tasks:

- transform and deliver products

- negotiate with partners

- exchange appropriate, timely, and updated information

- control costs and increase efficiency

- anticipate the needs of customers

- react to customer feedback

- provide a fair return to shareholders.

Competitive pressures and customer expectations are pushing organizations into addressing two factors that govern the performance of the supply chain. The first is speed (velocity), which refers to a company's ability to keep pace with continuously transforming market conditions, varying customer expectations, customized product features and collaborative partner networks. The second is variability, which concerns how well an organization can respond to changes in customer orders relating to destination or content – right up to or even during shipment – and how responsive it is to changes in demand forecasts or technical engineering updates.

Average organizations address variability, as it applies to order administration and handling issues, by improving their forecasting processes. Best-in-class enterprises are prepared to make more substantial changes. They not only use forecasting, but also adapt their business structures and supply chains in order to become more agile.

In my research into the evolution of supply chain management I have encountered many successful organizations that seek to control velocity and variability in the supply chain by leveraging a third factor that governs the performance of the value chain – visibility. Imagine you are driving a car on a busy road. Only when you have perfect road visibility can you accurately assess traffic conditions, decide when to speed up (velocity) and change direction (variability) in order to avoid the traffic jams and reach your destination as quickly and safely as possible.

Improving visibility in their supply chains enables enterprises to build competitive advantage. It allows them to determine the strategic advantages and disadvantages of many possible actions that might shape their final offering to their customers. These actions include not only activities within a company, but also the external activities of distribution and disposal/return which occur at the level of the supplier or consumer.

Greater visibility in the supply chain makes it easier for an organization to better understand which segments, distribution channels, price points, product differentiation, selling propositions and value chain configurations – such as the linkages between activities and processes that occur within and outside the company – will yield the greatest increase in competitive advantage.

Applying the New Definition of Visibility

Inventory visibility is a particularly important aspect, as supply chain solutions are primarily determined by their ability to manage logistics, material handling, inventory management and shop-floor processes. Nevertheless there is a need to look beyond inventory management to redefine visibility. Most successful organizations now consider four key factors that make up supply chain visibility:

1. *Product visibility.* This relates mainly to data on item definition, localization, life cycle and quality. Within this definition are enterprise software solutions covering bill-of-material management, track-and-trace identification, product configuration, product life cycle and product quality.

2. *Process visibility.* This enables the cross-referencing and control of the many operations that occur within an organization. It includes planning operations such as supply chain network design, customer demand forecasting, production planning, capacity management and maintenance planning. Manufacturing operations – production scheduling, shop-floor control, work-in-progress, track-and-trace and production efficiency also come under this definition, as do purchasing processes, such as spend management, supplier performance evaluation and real-time monitoring of process phases. Performance analyzes – including plant operational analysis, awareness of activities within any given plant, comprehensive category and product-level analysis across the entire supply chain – are further key elements, as are billing and invoicing, and returns logistics processes.

3. *Partner visibility.* This enables organizations to understand customers' value propositions and communicate them to internal functions and to suppliers. It allows them to create supplier portfolios based on pre-set target margins for each product or service, which are then used to better understand and negotiate margins and profitability in the light of how these are influenced by suppliers' services. Many organizations are adopting supplier cost-breakdown analysis to estimate the 'fair' return they should give their suppliers, which provides higher-level verification of processes within the supply chain. Organizations can then focus on the big picture, rather than on micro-managing pennies. Contract compliance, customer relationship management, global trade management and channel relationship management are among many solutions that support and enable better partner visibility.

4. *Profit visibility.* This is the measurement of the impact of supply chain operations on profitability, showing how they affect the

bottom line. It requires an appropriate set of indicators, and basic financial drivers are a good starting-point for a personalized – though generally acceptable – performance measurement system. Different departments within an organization handle the inbound and outbound elements of the supply chain. And, at some point in the middle, profit visibility determines how well the customer value proposition is communicated from one to the other. Solutions include supply chain operations reference metrics, economic value-added models, enterprise asset management solutions, cost-information benchmarks, enterprise profit optimization and best practices such as those put forward by Pittiglio Rabin Todd & McGrath (PRTM), the American Productivity and Quality Center (APQC) and the Centre for Advanced Purchasing Studies (CAPS).

If an organization focuses solely on visibility of the manufactured product as it progresses through the supply chain, it misses out on the opportunity to ensure that its strategic goals are closely aligned to the objectives of its supply chain processes. This gap can be closed relatively easily by adding the additional categories of visibility – process, partner and profit.

Supply Chain Management Imperatives

Clearly, supply chain management is changing and organizations need to re-evaluate what the supply chain can deliver in terms of value. They must also recognize the need to invest time and resources in changing their structure, processes and technology in order to fully capitalize on the opportunities that supply chain management offers. A clear picture of the potential added value can be obtained by expanding forecasting activities into a more collaborative approach to planning which takes into account both the demand side and the supply side of an organization.

Supply chain managers need to examine how technology can help them to move towards this increasingly collaborative environment and to secure buy-in from senior executives to make the necessary investment happen. Furthermore, they must adapt their definition of visibility in the supply chain to encompass processes, partners and profitability in order to attain a more comprehensive view of how all the elements of a supply chain interact to affect their overall performance.

2

Supply Chain Management as a Strategic Corporate Asset

Supply chain management can help a company achieve the true return on investment of customer relationship management (CRM) systems, making it easier to see how well-managed and efficient supply chain operations have a significant bearing on the organization's overall performance. One important benefit is that supply chain management reduces the time required for a new product or service to progress from the initial concept to its final delivery to the market. Indeed, a key objective of supply chain management is to bring new ideas to market faster, whether they are innovations from in-house or ideas gleaned from elsewhere that an enterprise needs to transform into deliverable products faster than its competitors. Because it is the gateway to the market for any business, supply chain management adds value to the time an organization spends developing new products and services. This chapter demonstrates that the value of corporate time is the currency of supply chain management and that this justifies its definition as a strategic corporate asset.

Alongside the time benefits delivered by supply chain management, we will look at some of the emerging models that illustrate the strategic importance of the supply chain, such as bionomics and the red ocean/blue ocean theory. From this platform I will also demonstrate that poor supply chain performance destroys shareholder value, by looking at how supply chain management directly affects income statements and balance sheets. Seeing supply chain management's impact on financial measurement is the first step towards improving the dialogue between the finance function and supply chain managers.

Finally, we will examine how current thinking about supply chain management is changing in line with the perceptions of its growing importance and how this is increasing the need for finance and supply chain management to communicate in a common language.

Delivering the Value of Corporate Time

Supply chain management profoundly affects the length of time involved in carrying out the processes that take place within a company's existing functions – such as sales, marketing, purchasing, production and warehousing – and across the entire network of stakeholders in the supply chain, including its customers and service providers. Supply chain decisions account for the time required for customer activity. Furthermore, supply chain management assumes that this time has a cost attached.

The purpose and function of the supply chain comes down to a simple mantra: deliver the right product – or service – in the right place, at the right time and in the right condition. Traditional interpretations of this have led many corporate executives to see supply chain management solely as a set of activities dedicated to moving material and information around the supply chain network, with a particular focus on three principal factors:

1.   a low-cost supplier base

2.   a reduced asset base

3.   network management.

If we re-evaluate this definition, however, it becomes obvious that each of its elements can be viewed as affecting the value of corporate time.

The Right Product or Service

A product or service must be one for which the market is ready and waiting. For instance, if a company launches a new DVD, delivering the right product means making sure that this particular item – and only this item – is ready when the market expects it. An interesting comparison is the counterfeit market for DVDs where delivery must be even timelier. In this case, the movie has to be one that consumers want to purchase at that particular time and its supply must beat the legal supply chain with which it competes. While (low) price is certainly the main consideration for a purchase decision, the availability of the counterfeited good must be ensured. Whilst I certainly do not condone this illegal practice, the observation of the logistics behind such a black market highlights the importance of time-to-market, especially in terms of the constraints under which it has to perform.

Other factors, such as marketing promotions, can influence the timing of the right product. Retailers must choose products for promotion well in advance to ensure that customers will buy them when they are made available. Making sure that the right products are sold will depend heavily on the forecasting that backs up any promotional activity. The more rapidly a company reacts to changes (velocity – the time factor governing the sale of any product or service), the less inventory needs to be stocked to hedge for uncertainties. Velocity is driven by visibility, as discussed in Chapter 1.

In the Right Place

As well as being physically available to consumers at the right time, a product or service must be transferred across all the nodes of the supply chain network well in advance in order to be in the right place when needed. The right place must also be determined well in advance, and all parties of the supply chain network must be synchronized in order to move the goods, or enable the service, so that it can reach its final destination. Achieving effective synchronization requires a properly designed supply chain, with all of its constituent nodes established beforehand to ensure delivery to the final and right destination. Furthermore, transit times must be factored in to achieve delivery at the right place since infrastructure constraints and congestion can delay deliveries and increase the complexity of the supply chain. Note that time is a vital element at all stages of ensuring that a product or service arrives at its correct destination.

There are many examples of transit times causing delays. One retailer in the clothing industry lamented the delays in getting goods through US West Coast ports, further compounded by hold-ups caused by a lack of capacity in the intermodal transport and haulage sectors.[1] The retailer, despite using larger, faster ships to transport goods, was losing a minimum of three days in transit – time it could ill afford given that the fashion industry is highly time-sensitive. Enterprises want to make ordering decisions at the last possible

---

1   L. Harrington, 'Logistics at the C-Level: Are We There Yet?', *Inboundlogistics.com*, June 2005, at: http://www.inboundlogistics.com/articles/features/0605_feature02.shtml.

moment, relying on fast, efficient delivery. In this case, problems with the transport infrastructure put the retailer in an awkward position, forcing it to ask its merchants to place orders earlier than they would like. Delays in the logistics process result in poor customer service, which affects strategy and competitive performance. They are, therefore, a concern for senior executives.

The ability of the supply chain to operate in a timely manner and to deliver a product or service in the right place is also affected by how well a company can manage all aspects of compliance with regulatory standards, including those that specifically apply to the final delivery destination. This final destination – the right place – may well have specific regulatory constraints to take into account. For instance, local requirements in terms of documentation may mean that a company has to make specific provisions for the time needed to process documentation accompanying shipped products.

At the Right Time

From the supply chain perspective, determining the right time means balancing the expectations of sales and marketing with the demands of operations. Any new product or service that is brought to market – the market being the right place – must not overlap or be in conflict with existing products or services. If the timing of a new product's introduction to the market is not synchronized with the equivalent 'right' time for the disposal of expiring goods already on the market, product cannibalization can be the highly dangerous end result.

There are many examples of supply chain models that aim to bring the product to market at the right time by balancing the expected delivery time, which is always too short, with operations times. These include make-to-stock (MTS), make-to-order (MTO) and engineer-to-order (ETO), and they all cover the processes involved in the sourcing, production and transportation of goods. To achieve delivery at the right time a company must also match its perceptions of customer requirements with the perceived value of the product or service. Mismatching these elements might prevent a company from achieving delivery at the right time. A food producer, for instance, might have focused on achieving a 99 per cent value in its on-time-in-full (OTIF) performance along the supply chain, but if it only manages to cook 76 per cent of its products to its consumers' preferences, its delivery performance could be severely undermined.

In the Right Condition

The time factor relating to delivering goods and services in the right condition can best be expressed by looking at the example of retail-ready packaging. This is a new packaging technique that allows product packaging to be used as part of the shelf display, eliminating the need to open boxes or repackage for display when the goods are first delivered to the retail outlet. Retail-ready packaging ensures that goods are delivered in the right condition, thereby reducing the time-to-display. It is used by both retail stores and retail goods producers and consists of containers and packaging for retail goods which are ready to be displayed instantly or with minimal set-up for retail consumption. Examples of retail-ready packaging are the cardboard boxes holding several packs of gum which are placed near the cash registers at supermarkets and retail stores. This is crucial in the fast-moving consumer goods (FMCG) sector. For retail and grocery outlets such as supermarkets, for example, a lack of product on the shelf is equivalent to a lost sale.

Of course, the displayable container must ensure that the quality and safety of the goods are in no way compromised. At the same time it must also be easy for the retailer to open and must have eye-catching graphics to ensure that the product meets the expectations of the marketing department. Finally, the product must be easy to use for the customer who purchases it. Achieving all of these qualities in one product requires that all those who play a role in the engineering chain be closely aligned and well synchronized.

It is not only in markets such as FMCG that the supply chain can have a significant impact on corporate time and the innovation which improved time value can support. The public sector, too, can benefit. The UK Office of Government Commerce (OGC), for instance, has advised contracting authorities that improvements in efficiency and transparency in the management of public-sector supply chains should be given due consideration.[2] The OGC highlights the advantages of analyzing supply chain management operations when allocating risk within an organization, which is vital in today's markets where the process of delivering goods and services is becoming far more complex. It also notes that focusing on supply chain management practices can reveal better opportunities for subcontracting.

---

2   Office of Government Commerce, 'Supply Chain Management in Public Sector Procurement: A Guide', at: http://www.ogc.gov.uk/documents/supply chain management_final_june05.pdf.

Key to the OGC's recommendations, however, is the scope for innovation along the entire supply chain, which could result in improved quality of service delivery and lower costs. Supply chain management can support innovation and link creative thinking at one stage to all other elements in the chain, allowing its benefits to be more fully realized.

To achieve these benefits the OGC also recognizes that it is crucial to consider supply chain management in the early stages of defining business needs, as this will clarify what is required to deliver a service more efficiently and effectively, and allow more appropriate targets for the development of delivery processes to be set.

There are many variables that, when examined in the light of supply chain management, clearly show that supply chain operations can have a major impact on the value of corporate time. We will examine these factors, which include days inventory outstanding (DIO), days sales outstanding (DSO), and days purchasing outstanding (DPO), later. For now, it is sufficient to appreciate that all three indicators quantify the value of time for an organization. We will come to see how the operation of the supply chain has a significant impact on these variables, which will further justify a view of the supply chain as the gateway to improving overall business performance.

Supply Chain Management Evolves to Influence Business Strategy

If we take a step back and view the supply chain from a different perspective, as should any senior executives with a view to ensuring the future success of their companies, it soon emerges that it is not only a tool for delivering goods and services, but also the physical expression of the long-term business strategy nurtured in the board room. The supply chain manager's mission is to translate a new corporate business vision into specific new objectives for the supply chain.

The effect of supply chain management on time factors at each stage of the supply chain, and the value of that time to the enterprise in terms of innovation and customer satisfaction, suggest that supply chain management should be considered at a much earlier stage in the planning of major projects and initiatives than is currently the norm. But first a business must decide what supply chain management is. Does it relate solely to logistics? Or to procurement? Or perhaps to distribution?

The supply chain can in fact be viewed much more broadly. It is an extension of the enterprise that crosses the boundaries of a single firm to involve a large number of diverse organizations. It is significantly larger than can be appreciated by focusing on a single element, such as logistics.

Warren Hausman, Professor of Operations Management in the Department of Management Science and Engineering at Stanford University, states: 'The battleground of the next decade will be supply-chain versus supply-chain.'[3] This statement has profound implications for how firms should approach the measurement of supply chain performance, given that they must take into account the needs and performance of a growing number of stakeholders, each with different goals and capabilities.

While its key business goal may still be to reduce costs, supply chain management is now also perceived as a key business enabler and, as such, gets far more attention from corporate level (C-level) executives. In today's business world there are new forces at play that have changed the way in which enterprises look at their supply chains: declining retail prices, increasing upstream costs – including fuel, materials and overheads – the increasing emphasis on profitable growth, the trend towards globalization, security and the greater demands of regulatory compliance all generate new pressures that force businesses to develop new ways of working. Putting these new processes into practice cannot be achieved without a keen eye on the supply chain.

The primary challenge for senior management is growth, often measured on a very short timescale, so executives are starting to show more interest in supply chain management to find out how it can truly benefit their businesses. Leading thinkers on the subject of supply chain management are now focused on how best to align internal structures and external organizations to maximize the revenues derived from the overall management of the product life cycle. As a result, new business models are emerging, in which issues concerning the supply chain are taking on far greater prominence than ever before.

New Models: Blue Oceans, Red Oceans and Bionomics

As supply chain managers develop new models and adapt existing ones, they must remain open to new thinking and make the effort to innovate around supply chain processes. Some emerging models demand a lot of work on

---

3   W.H. Hausman, *Supply Chain Performance Metrics*, New York: Springer, 2006 p. 1.

the part of the supply chain manager, given that they diverge radically from traditional thinking.

One such technique that has received a lot of publicity is the Blue Ocean Strategy, originally developed by Professor W. Chan Kim and Professor Renée Mauborgne, research partners and members of the faculty at INSEAD, an international graduate business school. It begins by recognizing that for a long time companies have fought for competitive advantage, market quota and differentiation, but goes on to note that in today's overcrowded markets direct competition may lead only to a bloody 'red ocean' where rivals fight tooth and nail in a space that offers ever-shrinking profit margins. The new strategy put forward by Kim and Mauborgne suggests that success is achieved not by trying to win in direct competition, but rather by creating 'blue oceans' of untapped demand within mature markets into which they can successfully grow. The research concludes that the way to win against competitors is to stop fighting them on the same terms.

Red oceans represent all existing business sectors and they are well known to all the companies that operate in them. Boundaries between sectors are well defined and accepted by competing organizations, and all parties know the rules of competition. In such an environment companies try to overcome competitors to acquire a bigger portion of the existing demand, and, because those markets are becoming increasingly crowded, the potential for growth and profit is continuously shrinking. Products rapidly become commoditized, and fierce competition turns the ocean red with the blood of competing enterprises.

Blue oceans represent all the business sectors that do not yet exist – they are the unknown and untapped markets that an enterprise could potentially exploit. In finding blue oceans companies are moving into unexplored market spaces characterized by new sources of demand offering very profitable growth potential. In blue oceans competition is irrelevant because the rules of the game have yet to be defined.

Blue oceans are nothing new, although they have never been so clearly labelled before. Untapped markets have always existed. In fact, economies always expand into new markets, proving that there is an incredible capacity to create new sectors and to innovate within existing ones. This is proven simply by looking at the Standard Industry Classification (SIC) and its replacement in 1997 by the North American Industry Classification System (NAICS). The

SIC previously covered ten industry sectors, but NAICS expanded that to 20 in order to reflect a business landscape that is constantly growing into new industrial arenas.

There are many forces driving this expansion and the consequent need to create more blue oceans. Advances in technological capability, for instance, have substantially improved productivity in many industries, often resulting in situations where supply exceeds demand. The race towards globalization, as well as the introduction of the euro that has made prices in Europe more transparent, exacerbates this problem. As soon as trade barriers come down and information on products and prices is instantly and globally available, the standardization of products and services accelerates, leading to ever more intense price wars and falling profit margins.

Escaping the red oceans of bloody competitive war to explore blue oceans of new demand requires a major shift in mindset from the traditional 'company-centric' perspective that seeks the prerequisites for success within the characteristics of a single enterprise. There are no examples of companies that have perpetually achieved high profitability. All have times when they excel and times when they suffer, which suggests that the 'company' is not the best unit of analysis for exploring the potential success of a new business strategy.

A more appropriate unit of analysis suggested by the authors of the blue ocean/red ocean model is the 'strategic move' – the combination of managerial actions and decisions taken when proposing a business model that creates a new market. Strategy is the key factor that determines the successful creation of a blue ocean. Beating the competition is no longer the benchmark for success. Instead, value innovation takes precedence.

VALUE INNOVATION

Value innovation is created when the organizations' actions positively influence both its cost structure and its value proposition to customers. Cost savings derive from the reduction or elimination of competitive factors in a particular market sector. The value to the buyer increases through the creation or improvement of those elements that have never before been offered to the market. As time passes, costs are further reduced through economies of scale, which are generated by the higher sales volumes resulting from an increase in supply.

When discount retailers take up a large amount of space in a market, companies can pursue innovative product lines that generate higher margins rather than getting into heated competition over low-margin items. 'Keep and improve the good things. Throw away the bad' can be assumed as the motto of such a strategy. Limited Brands is one organization that has recognized this. Realizing that it lacked the necessary supply chain technologies and processes to constantly sustain the required speed-to-market to compete in the offer of new merchandising, it set about restructuring its organization to relieve stores of logistics and processing tasks (that is, 'throw away the bad'), putting in place a logistics information system (that is, 'keep and improve the good things') to provide the necessary visibility and control to support its business growth strategy.[4]

Focusing on value innovation mandates companies to orient themselves towards achieving a leap in value, but this can only be accomplished when they align the goals of innovation with usefulness, price and cost. If innovation is not anchored to value in this way, market pioneers and technology companies, for example, will all too often lay golden eggs only for competitors to steal them. An obvious example of this comes from the games console market. Sony's problems in getting its PlayStation 3 to market allowed Microsoft and Nintendo to pick up extra sales as a result.

BIONOMICS AND PUNCTUATED EQUILIBRIUM

The business imperatives that are driving the need for organizations to consider new business models can be classified as the disruptive events in an industry ecosystem, which require new species of enterprises to evolve to fill areas of previously unfulfilled market demand. This terminology is appropriate, given that the situation very much resembles the dynamics described in the analytical model known as bionomics.[5]

The concept of bionomics is based on the assumption that a parallel can be drawn between an ecosystem based on genetic information and an economy determined by technical information. Essentially, it examines economic relationships among organisms in relation to their environments. To understand the model better it is useful to look at our understanding of the process of evolution in the natural world. In his discussion of bionomics Rothschild

---

4   B.J. Gibson, S.M. Rutner and K.B. Manhodt, 'How Trigger Events Can Get the CEO's Attention', *Supply Chain Management Review*, 1 November 2005.
5   M. Rothschild, *Bionomics: Economy as Ecosystem*, New York: Holt, 1990.

describes how some of the problems left open by Darwin's theory are to some extent resolved by the theory of Punctuated Equilibrium. This not only holds that evolution does not happen overnight, but also challenges the conventional view that it is a process that happens steadily over millions of years.

Bionomics goes along with an emerging view that evolutionary change occurs in a sequence of relatively short bursts, each of which may span some hundred thousands of years. It also suggests that a species does not change once it is established, but reaches equilibrium – provided that its form is still appropriate to the environment in which it exists. Should its environment change, however, a species will migrate in order to find new ecological conditions to which it is better suited. The theory also contends that smaller groups will separate from the main population and may find other benign environments in which they can continue to exist. In such a model it may be concluded that, in circumstances where the environment continues to change, such splinter groups may develop advantages over the original populations from which they split. This could ultimately result in these offshoot groups returning to their original territory as invaders, competing aggressively with their parent population and potentially causing their extinction because of the advantages gained by choosing a different evolutionary path.

If we take this theory of Punctuated Equilibrium and transpose it on to the ecosystem of modern organizations we might conclude that those enterprises which do not feel the need to evolve in line with the developing dynamics of constantly changing markets – in other words, those companies which adopt the 'if ain't broke, don't fix it' approach to business – are doomed to extinction and may be replaced by more adaptive and resistant species of enterprise.

In order to remain successful, companies must possess the openness and perspicacity to heed the signs which may foretell events that will disrupt their ecosystem. They must be ready not only to adapt once a cataclysmic event has occurred, but also to take the risk of exploring areas that appear to be merely niches or even hostile environments during the periods of stability and relative tranquillity that precede such disruption.

Cataclysmic events do sometimes occur, and one of the next major disruptions will probably come when companies become more insistent that the results from their supply chains be precisely measured and start to quantitatively anticipate the value that supply chain management can create. The real disruption will not stem from the fact that such a request is made, but from the completely new way in which people working in the supply chain will have to measure value. Only those companies that know how to blend their knowledge of supply chain practices and execution with financial rigour are likely to survive in a new ecosystem that will place more emphasis on measuring the direct impact of supply chain management on shareholder value.

The Threat to Shareholder Value

Strong supply chain management practices can reduce operating costs and help organizations control the costs of their logistics function. In recent years, when economic circumstances have often been challenging, executives have demanded cost reduction and savings throughout their organizations. Supply chain managers have responded to these demands by taking the lead in delivering what collectively amounts to billions of dollars of savings in inventories, freight costs, procurement and other costs associated with logistics. Furthermore, almost every company has enjoyed bottom-line benefits as a result of these diligent practices without having to endure any significant disruption to their overall organizational ecosystems. Although CEOs no longer view cost reduction as their primary goal – their focus having moved towards the creation of profitable growth – supply chain and logistics managers are not yet mobilizing themselves in support of this new goal. The main reason for this can be found, not surprisingly, in the fact that they have become too comfortable focusing on cost savings and feel much less at ease promoting top-line benefits, particularly as the evidence suggests that they are still unsure about how they should go about achieving them.

There is a general tendency to dismiss as too nebulous those investments in supply chain personnel, processes and technology that cannot be proven to be key drivers in achieving competitive advantage and, therefore, profitable growth. Many corporate-level executives have not yet understood the intrinsic connection between supply chain competency and corporate performance, and as a result they are unable to appreciate the true value of investment in the supply chain. In many organizations executives are unaware of the benefits of enhancing supply chain management, so long as supply chain operations continue to run smoothly. Research sponsored by the Council of Supply Chain Management Professionals puts forward evidence that points to a distinct lack of interest among senior management: 'No one cares about supply chain management until there is a problem.'[6]

6   K.B Manrodt, B.J. Gibson and S.M. Rutner, 'Learn How to Talk the CEO-Talk: Communicating the Value of Supply Chain Management to your CEO', *Supply Chain Management Review*, July 2005.

Research continues into attitudes at C-level, but so far it seems as though the broad range of responsibilities that senior executives are required to handle impedes their ability – and willingness – to become involved with supply chain management issues except in sporadic bursts when a specific problem demands their attention. For that reason supply chain professionals must be ready to deliver value through their own initiatives in order to support their companies' strategic vision. If they can show tangible contributions to the overall performance of their enterprises, this will provide a valuable showcase for supply chain management, help to make it clear what effect it can have on the organization and enhance the perception of the value of the supply chain among senior executives.

At their core, all successful business strategies have supply chain strategies that help build competitive advantage. There is a growing body of literature that analyses the main factors that contribute to shareholder value, which reflects a company's ability to generate profitable results through judicious and effective management of its operations. Profitable results are quantitatively measured by economic profit, which is defined as a single-period metric that determines the value created by a company in that period – usually a year – or alternatively as the net operating profit after tax less the equity charge, a risk-weighted cost of capital. We will discuss this calculation in more detail in Chapter 3, where we will examine the economic value-added tree.

The Influence of Supply Chain Management on Financial Measures

It is important to look in detail at the basic financial figures that make up the various elements of economic profit, on which supply chain management clearly has a significant impact. The key figures affected when glitches in supply chain operations arise can be identified as components of the income statement and balance sheet. The examples below, which focus on these components, clearly show that supply chain management does indeed influence corporate value.

Indicators of an organization's financial performance are already recognized as being the income statement and the balance sheet reports. The income statement measures profitability over a specific period of time, taking into account flows of revenue and expenses in order to calculate net profit for that period. It is a useful starting point for revealing the impact of supply chain activities during a specific period, whether from the perspective of sales or costs. It gives a valuable insight into how an organization generates its revenues and shows how margins can be eroded by both direct and indirect costs. A balance sheet provides a record of changes in assets and liabilities, which will partly be based on the activities that are outlined in the income statement. If a company wishes to track how current and long-term investments give rise to changes in its liabilities it can use its balance sheet to look at specific changes in inventories, cash, plant and equipment, accounts receivable and accounts payable.

There is also another data set that financial managers frequently use – the cash flow statement. This synthesizes the key components of the balance sheet and income statement by detailing the sources and uses of cash during the period measured on the income statement. The cash flow report essentially summarizes changes in the balance sheet and income statement accounts. Since the quantities tracked in the cash flow report derive from the balance sheet and income statement reports, we will concentrate on the latter two elements to illustrate the impact of supply chain management.

The Impact of Supply Chain Management on the Income Statement

Looking at the structure of the income statement, net income (also referred to as net operating profit after taxes – NOPAT) emerges as the main figure. Using Figure 2.1 as a reference, we can see the breakdown of NOPAT and appreciate that this financial result is obtained through the calculation of figures that directly depend on the performance of the supply chain.

SALES

Let us begin by looking at the first component of NOPAT – sales. Since we are focusing here on how poor supply chain performance destroys shareholder value, it is useful to identify possible supply chain glitches that can impact negatively on sales. The first example, which can be described as the 'usual suspect' in supply chain disruption, is when a company runs out of inventory. The effects of this can be dramatic. A study by Professor Vinod R. Singhal, Professor of Operations Management at the DuPree College of Management at Georgia Institute of Technology, found that supply chain glitches badly hit shareholder value. After adjusting for industry and market movements,

INCOME STATEMENT

Total net sales and revenue	193,517
Cost of sales and other expenses (COGS)	159,951
Selling, general and administrative expenses (SG&A)	20,394
Interest expense	11,980
Total costs and expenses	192,325
Income from continuing operations before income taxes, equity income and minority interests	1,192
Income tax (benefit) expense	(911)
Equity income and minority interests	702
Income from continuing operations	2,805
(Loss) from discounted operations	–
Gain on sale of discounted operations	–
Net income	2,805

Figure 2.1   Example of income statement report

the total shareholder value loss associated with a glitch can be as high as 25 per cent.[7]

Sales results can be affected by supply chain operations. Higher levels of customer retention lead to greater sales, which typically occur because customers are more likely to place a greater proportion of their purchases with a given supplier. One way in which supply chain glitches can negatively affect sales growth is when a company fails to dynamically shift production to owned or contracted facilities located in markets that have high retail prices for the products that are being manufactured. If a company wants to generate improved sales flows and supply a greater volume of products to customers showing high levels of demand, then it must show itself to be flexible, responsive and reliable in the delivery of those goods. Achieving that is heavily dependent on the quality of supply chain operations.

If it lacks flexibility a supply chain will not be sufficiently agile to respond to changes in the market, nor will it be able to gain or maintain competitive

7   V.R. Singhal, 'Quantifying The Impact of Supply Chain Glitches on Shareholder Value', SAP White Paper, 2003 at: http://www.sap.com/solutions/business-suite/scm/pdf/BWP_Quantify. pdf.

advantage. If it fails to be responsive, a company will find that the speed at which it can deliver products to the customer through the supply chain will decrease. If the supply chain is not reliable, a company will perform poorly in terms of delivering the right product to the right place, at the right time, in the right condition and packaging, in the right quantity, with the right documentation and to the right customer.

Supply chain management has a growing potential to be viewed as a front-office tool. Demand manifests itself through multiple channels, such as online marketplaces, as well as through partnerships. In each of these channels the supply chain can be a critical element in supporting the exchange of goods, information and funds. More and more margin potential is now being derived after a product is shipped. An Accenture study of the automobile industry revealed that sales of $9 billion in parts and services contributed $2 billion in profits at General Motors. By comparison, car sales of $150 billion produced earnings of just $1 billion for the company. In general, as the product margins fall, the service margins no longer dilute overall earnings. The total margin of product and service combined should remain in a 30–40 per cent range – not as heady as those 60–70 per cent margins the company enjoys when the product is the industry sensation, but far better than the 20 per cent that seems to be the product's destiny when it eventually loses its unique position in the marketplace. Service and support, therefore, are becoming just as important as the product itself. If the supply chain is to be at the heart of a company's profitable service and support processes, then it must ensure that it does not falter or fail in the face of the demands placed upon it.

SALES RETURNS AND ALLOWANCES

If we look at another component of NOPAT – sales returns and allowances – we can easily highlight another area where the supply chain must remain robust. Delayed deliveries are among the typical faults in supply chain management that impact on sales returns and allowances. There are many factors that can trigger the return of goods by a client, such as poor quality of product or service, incomplete or partial delivery of goods, incorrect quantities shipped, or incorrect product attributes – for example, when the colour, technical specifications or functionality of the product are wrong. The returns that these errors generate will ultimately reduce total sales figures. If a company chooses to offset the negative impact of these factors on customer satisfaction and loyalty by offering discounts or special prices, this will increase the allowance value and sales figures will be further eroded.

COST OF GOODS SOLD

Looking again at the income statement report (Figure 2.1), we encounter another component that builds the final value of NOPAT – cost of sales and other allowances, also known as cost of goods sold (COGS). This is an important figure, which describes the direct expenses incurred in producing a particular good for sale, including the actual cost of materials and direct labour costs associated with getting the product into a sellable condition. This figure is directly related to supply chain operations because the transactions and operations that add up to produce this figure are, per se, supply chain operations.

Supply chain glitches that impact on COGS can be easily tracked under the header of cost of materials. The purchase price of the goods or services is a result of negotiations between the purchasing department and the supplier's sales department. When an organization takes a myopic, silo-based approach to purchasing – where it remains separated from supply chain operations – it will not benefit from the organic and cross-departmental perspective that seeks to link supplier relationship management closely with the characteristics of an efficiently and effectively managed supply chain.

Interviews with corporate supply chain executives reveal that there are more ingredients that go into the negotiation of a purchase price than merely a mark-up added to the cost of making a product. The final price paid for a product or service must instead reflect the total investment required to perform a specific action or a series of actions, which means taking into account the purchase price plus the costs of all other activities along the supply chain. The purchase price may often represent only a fraction of the total cost. Those companies that achieve best practice in cost management take this into account and factor in all the costs associated not only with producing a product or service, but also with delivering it to their customers. Furthermore, they seek to introduce similar practices among their suppliers.

Current best practices in strategic sourcing encompass all the elements required to improve process quality and forecast accuracy. Organizations such as Harley-Davidson Motor Company have formed what they refer to as 'supplier councils', which are coordinated by the client's purchasing group and meet frequently throughout the year to discuss key strategic initiatives. At the other end of the spectrum are companies who have poor practices in this area and do not share savings with a supplier when that supplier has identified an area where costs could potentially be reduced and has proposed a method to realize those savings. This equates to a major glitch in supply chain management.

To avoid additional losses that might arise from mismanagement of the supply chain, organizations should initiate programmes that use value-added, stream-mapping models and other techniques that can be applied to supply chain processes, such as materials handling, warehouse management, production forecast planning, manufacturing operations management, inbound and outbound shipments, returns and post-sales operations management. Failing to run these programmes or implement such processes will not produce efficiency and productivity improvements, and this will inevitably affect direct labour expenses which constitute the other element of the COGS calculation. This further confirms that the full spectrum of constituent elements in the COGS calculation is directly mapped against activities that fall within the domain of supply chain management.

OPERATING EXPENSES

There is also another component that builds the NOPAT figure of the income statement – namely, operating expenses. Supply chain management activities that are registered under this heading usually occur in the back office. Many activities combine to produce the figure for operating expenses and they should all be duly registered if an enterprise is to avoid surprises or inexplicable hidden costs when it does its year-end budget. Failure to take account of all these activities could potentially lead to harmful disruption, particularly when the organization realizes that these expenses relate to activities that are as numerous and varied as those run on the shop floor, in warehouses, distribution centres and on trailer routes.

In order to more clearly define these activities it helps to use definitions and practices that derive from the Supply Chain Council's SCOR™ model.[8]

One of the first back-office processes that must be taken into account to properly measure operating expenses is the management of business rules during planning cycles. This refers to the process of establishing, maintaining and enforcing decision support criteria for supply chain planning, and includes activities such as the measurement of service levels against the service requirements laid down for trading partners and other stakeholders in the

---

8   See http://www.supply-chain.org/page.ww?section=SCOR+Model&name=SCOR+Model.

supply chain. If the demand planning function can be made more reliable, the flow of goods and funds along the supply chain will be much more stable and, consequently, the people responsible for running the supply chain will need less time to anticipate changes in demand. The outcome is a more responsive supply chain, which means less time spent on fire-fighting, as many potential problems will be headed off before they occur or will be tackled more quickly should they arise. This has been proven – to give but one example – by research conducted by EyeOn, a consulting firm that specializes in the delivery of planning and control solutions to complex organizations.[9] This research shows that an additional benefit of a more stable flow along the supply chain is reduced overtime in the production process.

Another potential source of hidden operating expenses is the planning of total inventory limits, which includes raw materials, work in process, finished and purchased finished goods. This also comes about when those responsible for the supply chain set to work on building replenishment and ownership models, product mix and stocking locations. As these people work on defining an integrated supply chain transportation strategy and maintaining the data that characterizes total supply chain transportation requirements, as well as the management of transporters both within an organization and with its trading partners, there is significant potential for operating expenses to increase.

The same is true of the process of defining, establishing, maintaining and enforcing business rules for sourcing, which are eventually translated into the guidelines and policies that govern how an organization conducts business within its own divisions and with external entities. These sourcing business rules may include, for example, the policies that cover supplier selection, negotiation of terms, fulfilment and delivery performance, as well as the definition of the terms for relationships at specific levels of collaboration and partnership.

A sizeable proportion of a company's operating resources is spent during the ongoing process of defining and maintaining a unique network of suppliers that can deliver a specific set of products. This category of expenses includes the fall-off in activity associated with establishing a new supplier relationship or restructuring a relationship with an existing supplier. This process involves many activities necessary to identify and qualify a supplier and to finalize the terms and conditions of sourcing. In addition, operating costs are run up during the process of managing supplier certification, which not only involves

---

9   'Improved Forecast Accuracy Does Pay Back!', 2005, at: http://www.eyeon.nl/index. php?id=68&id2=363.

certifying new suppliers, but also maintaining the current status of existing supplier relationships. Another significant, and frequently underestimated, contributor to operating expenses is the set of activities related to managing existing purchase orders or supplier contracts. This includes processes such as the management of volume pricing, enforcing terms and conditions, resolving problems and maintaining an accurate picture of the status of such purchase orders or contracts.

There are also other important key tasks, such as establishing, maintaining and enforcing rules for the management of production details, which include part/item master, bills of materials/formulas, routings, processes, equipment requirements and tooling, as well as other information that specifies the method of production for any given product. These usually go hand in hand with the process of specifying, maintaining and disposing of manufacturing capital assets, including repairs, alterations, calibration and many other tasks necessary to maintain the production capabilities of the fixed asset base that supports the manufacturing function. The same is true of the continuous management of activities that ensure equipment and facilities are maintained in proper order.

All the factors mentioned above that contribute to the final figure for operating expenses are related to activities that occur within an organization. They constitute additional day-to-day duties for those involved in managing the supply chain, who are generally more focused on managing collaboration with external partners. This includes collecting, maintaining and communicating information to support delivery planning and execution, from order data – such as customer preferences, order history, status and delivery requirements – to warehouse data, transportation data and delivery data. Similarly, we must account for all activities linked to establishing and maintaining finished goods, inventory limits or levels, replenishment models, ownership, product mix and stocking locations.

Finally, two further components contribute to the final figure of operating expenses. First, there is the process of defining and maintaining the network of distribution channels for a specific product line. Second is the management of import/export requirements, such as recording and maintaining regulations and rates which constrain the process of ordering and delivering products. This may also include determining customs requirements and establishing terms and conditions for letters of credit.

DEPRECIATION, INTEREST EXPENSES AND INCOME TAXES

Other components of the NOPAT figure that must also be considered when examining the impact of the supply chain on the financial performance of an enterprise are depreciation, interest expenses and income taxes. It may seem natural to consider these as purely financial elements, but, with just a little investigation using hypothetical glitches in the supply chain as before, we soon see that supply chain management can have a significant bearing on these elements of the income statement report.

Let us consider depreciation first. Assets that have a finite lifespan will lose value over time. In accounting, depreciation and its related concept, amortization, which is generally defined as the depreciation of intangible assets, are terms used to describe any method for attributing cost to an asset across its useful lifespan. An asset is an economic resource that an organization controls as a result of past transactions or events and from which future economic benefits may be obtained. Both current and fixed assets are normally the top component of a balance sheet report (see Figure 2.2, p. 43). An incorrect demand forecast – which is a typical supply chain glitch – triggers poor planning of production quantities that in turn leads to a poor schedule of supplies. Company equipment and resources, inventory, shop-floor space and company assets are therefore utilized in a way that affects the depreciation rate very differently from how it is set out in the company budget. Moreover, when considering assets and depreciation we find the first connection between income statement and balance sheet items and the performance of supply chain management operations as direct enablers of future performance.

Interest expenses and income taxes are apparently items that are affected by financial – that is to say non-operational – activities. There is a vast amount of literature covering supply chain management in terms of the optimization of inventory policies, network design, routing patterns and the allocation of resources. Researchers and practitioners have tended to focus on the operational side of an enterprise's activities. Some have put forward linkages between supply chain management and accounting, corporate finance and international tax law, but usually in a rather fragmented fashion. In fact there are currently no models that effectively integrate supply chain management and financial management, principally because none of the models proposed so far effectively consider the close coupling of production decisions with cash flow movements, royalty fees and dividend repatriations.

An interesting paper written by Morris Cohen and Arnd Huchzermeier states:

> *The current state-of-the-art in global manufacturing strategy planning models can be characterized by two fundamental approaches: network flow models and option valuation models. Network flow models exploit primarily portfolio effects within the firm's global supply chain network. In general, network structure decisions are numerous, but are exercised rather infrequently, e.g. on a periodic base. Alternatively, option value models focus primarily on production switching or sourcing decisions contingent on future states of nature. In general, production options are limited, but can be exercised frequently, e.g. on a continuous basis. The polarization in research is due to the analytical complexities of each modelling approach, i.e. network complexity in the first case and stochastic complexity in the second case. Consequently, there persists a significant gap in the literature on unified modeling approaches for global manufacturing strategy options under exchange risk.*[10]

In modern supply chain process management we find non-operational factors that strongly impact on the performance of supply chain activities. There have been attempts to extend supply chain management using financial management reference models and analysis. The most significant models, which are clearly correlated to the global, cross-border nature of current supply networks, are accomplished by relating supply chain management and financial management to opportunities that must dynamically respond to changes in market prices, demand and foreign exchange rates. They find that it is mainly foreign currency exchange-rate risk that has a significant effect on interest expenses and income taxes.

The design of the supply chain must be clearly framed by considering such factors as a strategic vision, the desired level of risk, competitive positioning and the characteristics of the industry in which it operates. On the whole, these factors are not considered to be components of supply chain management models, which are generally focused on reducing costs and do not take into account any consequences of the firm's ownership structure. Instead, the focus is usually on the costs arising from logistics – like transportation, duties and inventory – with highly leveraged factors, such as taxes, often overlooked.

---

10 M. Cohen and A. Huchzermeier, 'Global Supply Chain Management: A Survey of Research and Applications', in S. Tayur, R. Ganeshan and M. Magazine (eds), *Quantitative Models for Supply Chain Management*, Boston, MA: Kluwer Academic Press, 1999, pp. 3–4.

Large, multinational organizations may be able to minimize tax by optimizing their ownership structure, for example, or by improving the design of the supply chain to better align it with the existing structure and place it in the best possible context for international tax and foreign exchange risk. Redesigning the supply chain could, for instance, entail matching the locations of production facilities with customers, which might mitigate a significant amount of the risk from currency fluctuations.

Integrating finance management guidelines with supply chain design can help determine which production facilities or suppliers should be used to manufacture a particular product. There are a number of tactical tax management considerations that can be used to improve planning and operations. For example, in cases where there are potentially multiple sources for a given set of products, making changes to production sourcing can reduce income taxes. This can be done – albeit not easily – by dynamically shifting the production of low-margin products to high-tax jurisdictions, while shifting production of high-margin products to low-tax jurisdictions.

There are also ways in which well-implemented supply chain management operations can impact on interest expenses. A reduction in inventory value, for example, reduces the amount of capital tied up in stocks by reducing the so-called inventory carrying cost. This is a figure calculated by taking into account elements of inventory management such as storage, handling, obsolescence, damage, administration, loss (for example, pilferage) which, if not duly factored, generate 'hidden costs' that tend to be discovered too late and adversely affect the company's overall results. Similarly, by improving demand planning, and thereby increasing the reliability of demand forecasts, companies can also improve their overall financial forecasts. This lowers the risk profile for their shareholders, thereby resulting in benefits derived from reduced values for the weighted cost of capital.

Globalization has brought new players to the supply chain management scene in the form of free-trade zones and foreign investment agencies. Manufacturers are increasingly taking advantage of the benefits that can be derived from locating plants inside national foreign-trade zones. These zones potentially offer significant financial advantages:

- exemption from corporate taxes for manufacturing companies

- free international transfer of earnings and revenues

- no duties or tariffs on goods imported from abroad

- direct sales allowed within the hosting country.

A company can potentially benefit from tax incentive schemes and financial assistance for industry by carefully selecting a number of locations in which to run their supply chain activities. Supply chain decisions can also affect excise tax exemption, which can be applied to supply chain related choices such as new machinery and equipment, inventory on goods in transit and raw materials used in manufacturing.

Supply chain decisions can also play a vital role in attracting financial assistance, which is increasingly offered in fast-growing economies, notably in East Asia, Arabian Gulf states and East Africa. Further positive impact on interest expenses and income taxes may also come from local government loans (that is, country loans) for the construction of buildings or for the purchase of manufacturing equipment. Furthermore, some countries may offer financial aid for the expansion of existing plants in areas where there are high rates of unemployment.

All these financial tools intended to provide incentives for investment clearly depend on supply chain decisions and strategies.

The Impact of Supply Chain Management on the Balance Sheet

Having seen how the quality of supply chain practices can positively or negatively affect the principal elements of the income statement, we can now look at how supply chain management impacts on the other key report used by the financial community, the balance sheet (see Figure 2.2).

ASSETS

As we have already seen, the top items of the balance sheet are a company's assets. These assets may be classified in many ways, and certain divisions are required by generally accepted accounting principles (GAAP), which vary from country to country. For our examples we will use the classification laid down by US GAAP.

Current assets   The first balance sheet component that we should consider is current assets. These comprise cash and other assets that a company expects

ASSETS

Cash and cash equivalents	35,993
Other marketable securities	**21,737**
Total cash and marketable securities	57,730
Finance receivables – net	199,600
Loans held for sale	19,934
Accounts and notes receivable (less allowances)	21,236
Inventories (less allowances)	12,247
Deferred income taxes	26,241
Net equipment on operating leases (less accumulated depreciation)	34,214
Equity in net assets of nonconsolidated affiliates	6,776
Property – net	39,020
Intangible assets – net	4,925
Other assets	57,680
Total assets	**479,603**

LIABILITIES AND STOCKHOLDERS' EQUITY

Accounts payable (principally trade)	28,830
Notes and loans payable	300,279
Post-retirement benefits other than pensions	28,111
Pensions	9,455
Deferred income taxes	7,078
Accrued expenses and other liabilities	77,727
Total liabilities	451,480
Minority interests	397
Stockholders' equity	942
Capital surplus (principally additional paid-in capital)	15,241
Retained earnings	14,428
Subtotal	30,611
Accumulated foreign currency translation adjustments	(1,194)
Net unrealized gains on derivatives	589
Net unrealized gains on securities	751
Minimum pension liability adjustment	(3,031)
Accumulated other comprehensive loss	(2,885)
Total stockholders' equity	27,726
Total liabilities and stockholders' equity	**479,603**

Figure 2.2   Example of balance sheet report

to be converted to cash, sold or consumed either within a year or within the current operating cycle. These assets are continually turned over in the course of normal business activity. To examine the different items categorized under this heading we must first break down the current assets figure into its major components in order to focus particularly on those that are affected – positively or negatively – by supply chain practices.

The first of these is the receivables element. The accounts receivable figure is one of a series of accounting transactions dealing with the billing of customers who owe money to a person, company or organization for goods and services that have been provided to the customer. It is the amount that customers owe a business and is usually reported as net of allowance for uncollectable accounts. To more accurately assess the impact of supply chain management operations on receivables, and to highlight once again the importance of supply chain management in terms of time value, it is useful to use figures for days sales outstanding (DSO).[11]

This figure represents the amount of time required to collect an outstanding bill and therefore measures the speed at which customers are invoiced and payment is received. The processes that contribute to this figure begin the moment a product is sold and include the billing of the customer and ultimately the receipt of payment and the banking of credit. The first of these steps relates to the sales function. By investigating how malfunctions in supply chain management operations affect the sales process we can better identify those areas in which supply chain management affects DSO and, therefore, accounts receivable.

The most obvious problems that may arise are that the product is not delivered, or it is delivered in the wrong quantity, with the wrong specifications or in the wrong package and is eventually returned in full. Further along the chain there may be instances where a distributor does not return money collected from selling a product or service. In addition, poor performance in the invoicing process, which may be due to factors such as the inclusion of incorrect information on delivery documents, will extend the length of time between sales and the collection of funds.

There are, of course, ways in which companies can remedy the negative impacts on DSO that arise from problems in the supply chain. If, for example, a company builds an infrastructure of resources and services to move – and

---

11   DSO = (average receivables/ net sales) × 365.

remain – closer to the customer, and provides more reliable transit times and shorter lead times, it will head off many of these potential problems. Also, looking at patterns in customers' payment histories can help forecast the timing of incoming payments, making it possible to calculate the time value of money when considering how profitable a delivery to a given customer is likely to be.

Inventory   Inventory is another component of the current assets figure that demands closer attention in terms of how it is affected by the performance of the supply chain. Inventory comprises the assets that are traded as part of a company's day-to-day business, and inventory value, as reported on the balance sheet, is usually the historical cost or fair market value, whichever is lower. This is known as the 'lower of cost or market' rule. Inventory management is the process of developing and implementing inventory policies to service unpredictable customer demand, given parameters such as service targets, budgets, out-of-stock probabilities and costs, as well as demand fulfilment rates.

In many cases, finished inventory is created too early in the supply process. It is the job of the supply chain manager to find ways of postponing the completion of a product in order to reduce the total amount of inventory in the pipeline and improve the flexibility of the delivery process. An interesting practice for postponing inventory comes from Yohyon van Zantwijk, who points out that finishing products in large batches creates a significant delay for distributors before they can re-order a given product. Furthermore, manufacturers face a long delay before they can produce more of a particular item:

> *The discrepancy between supply and demand introduces inventory risk in the supply chain. This is where push behaviour originates. To get rid of the products that end users will not absorb the manufacturer forces his distributors into buying more, partially through minimum order quantities, partially through point rebates. And distributors do the same to their retail customers, increasing the negative effect of such inventory push down the chain.*

> *Selling to the next link generates immediate administrative profit. Supplying products from one tier to another is perceived to be sales. A source of profit for the supplier is misleading from a true value creation perspective. As long as it is acceptable administrative behaviour to register a profit when a product is shipped to the next link in the supply chain, we will see artificial spikes in sales every end of the month, quarter, and year. This common behaviour to push inventory down the*

supply chain leads to a discrepancy between supply and demand, with lost sales and inventory redundancy as an end-effect.

Commercial intuition might tell that the chance of a product to be sold increases when the product is closer to the consumer. However this is true only for those products that are visibly presented in the store. They have indeed a higher probability to be sold. The same does not apply for the remainder of the inventory held in the warehouse.

All parties in a supply chain should realize that it is only the consumer who can generate cash flow.

The consequent practice that reduces the risk of transferring inventory from one party to another at zero value takes inspiration from observing that pushing down inventory reduces the chances of actually selling the product. All inventory that is not needed in a store to cover demand in the time between two deliveries has zero chance to be sold in that store, whereas this same product lying in a distribution centre could have been shipped to another store that may have had demand for that product in the same time span. Redundant inventory lying in a distribution centre can be sold in the entire service area of that distribution centre, whereas redundant inventory in a store will not be sold by definition, because the shelf is still filled with the product anyway.[12]

Having assessed the impact of supply chain management processes on accounts receivable by addressing the time factors associated with the way in which the supply chain functions we can take a similar approach to measuring supply chain management's impact on inventory value using the days inventory outstanding (DIO) indicator.[13]

The first question to ask is: what can go wrong in supply chain management that will affect inventory? There are many glitches that can occur, including:

- excess time required to receive and process items in the goods inwards department

- excess time required to move material in the factory

---

12   Y. van Zantwijk, *The Responsive Supply Chain* (2nd rev. edn), Emrys Publications, 2006.
13   DIO = (average inventory ÷ COGS) × 365.

- delays in managing purchase and sales orders

- excess time spent preparing merchandise

- low efficiency of the distribution channel

- poor demand forecast and planning

- incorrect parameters used to establish stock levels

- purchase goods based on price volumes instead of what is really needed

- adopting push versus pull manufacturing models

- no use of the postponement strategy

- poor capacity planning

- lack of effort to increase the reliability of demand planning.

It is generally accepted that lower levels of inventory result in two financial advantages – less capital is tied up in stock and less storage space is required, the latter impacting positively on plant, property and equipment (PP&E) costs. In fact, reduced need for storage frees up physical space, which can be either rented or sold as a real estate asset. Ideally, inventory policies should both meet customer demand and bring cash outflows in line with the firm's global cash position.

Given that disruption in the supply chain can extend DIO, it follows that good supply chain management practices can reduce DIO and improve inventory management.

Fixed assets   Logistics, by its very nature, requires a large number of fixed assets. Trucks, distribution centres and automated handling systems all require considerable investment. Also referred to as PP&E, these assets are purchased for continued and long-term use in generating profit. PP&E also includes land, buildings, machinery, furniture, tools and wasting resources such as timber and minerals, which are written off against profits over their anticipated lifetime by charging depreciation expenses, except in the case of land. The accumulated amount of depreciation is shown either on the balance sheet itself or in the accompanying notes.

Fixed assets are the set of resources – material, human, tangible and intangible – that have a bearing on the financial wealth of the organization, especially as they are used to keep a business running. They are also referred to as 'capital assets', 'real capital', 'capital goods' or 'means of production'. A capital good can be used in the production of other goods, hence being considered as a factor of production. It is also human-made, in contrast to land, which refers not only to naturally occurring resources such as geographical locations, but also to minerals. Lastly, some economists define a capital good as one that is not used up immediately in the production process, unlike raw materials or intermediate goods.

Once again, we must examine how potential disruptions in the supply chain can affect these fixed assets. Among the most obvious issues are:

- lengthy and ineffective implementation of a new warehouse management system

- missed consolidation of distribution centres

- inefficient review of the international distribution centre network to expand (or contract) the number of facilities

- creation of oversized infrastructure to support a multi-year expansion in domestic and international markets

- location of facilities in new countries with no consideration of foreign-exchange risk.

Again, the reverse logic applies that efficient supply chain management can optimize the availability and use of fixed assets.

CURRENT LIABILITIES

The balance sheet contains two distinct groups of important data that relate to a company's liquidity, solvency, return on assets, return on investment and return on equity – assets and liabilities. Assets, as we have seen, are what a company uses to operate its business, while liabilities are the sources that support these assets. A useful definition of liabilities for the purpose of financial accounting is to describe them as obligations arising from past transactions or events that, when settled, may result in the transfer or use of assets, provision of services or other economic benefits in the future.

Liabilities also have three essential characteristics. First, they encapsulate a duty or responsibility to others that requires settlement by the future transfer or use of assets, provision of services or other economic benefits, at a specified or determinable date, on the occurrence of a specified event or on demand. Second, this responsibility takes the form of an obligation, with very little scope for an entity to avoid complying with its conditions. Third, the transaction or event that obligates the entity in question should already have occurred. Current liabilities are those that can reasonably be expected to be liquidated within one year.

Accounts payable   As we have done with previous financial items, we must first break down current liabilities into their constituent parts in order to understand how supply chain management practices influence them. The first item to consider is accounts payable and, once again, it is useful to use a time-related figure – in this case, days purchasing outstanding (DPO)[14] – to better understand the impact of supply chain management operations on accounts payable.

Note here that we again have a link between balance sheet and income statement components, in this case in the form of COGS, just as we did when we looked at depreciation. COGS provides a better representation of the cost of purchased materials, which are the basis for calculating DPO.

By focusing on the supply chain management practices that impact on DPO we indirectly assess another financial figure – cash-to-cash cycle time[15] – which has already become a significant feature of supply chain management. It represents the delay between payment for raw materials and the receipt of cash generated by selling final goods.

If the cash-to-cash cycle time is short (that is, the time to collect receivables is almost equivalent to the time to issue payments), a company can reasonably consider itself to be managing its working capital well. If the cycle time is long, a company must conclude that its capital spends too much time tied up in its

---

14   $DPO = (AP \div COGS) \times 365$.

15   Cash-to-cash cycle time = (days of inventory + days of receivables) – DPO.

business operations, which means that it cannot be used for other purposes such as investing in key parts of the business. There are even examples of companies that operate strategies, such as just-in-time inventory or extended credit terms, which can generate a negative value for the cash-to-cash cycle time, whereby they receive payments from the sale of products to customers before they are required to pay their suppliers.

The link between supply chain management operations and cash-to-cash cycle time becomes clear when a company realizes that the longer its cash remains tied up in inventories (that is, in raw materials, work in process and finished goods) the greater the time required for its production process and, consequently, the bigger the delay in receiving payment from customers. This is expressed through a higher value of accounts receivable. If a company can emulate those enterprises that have negative cash-to-cash cycle times by, for instance, pushing back the date at which it is required to pay for its raw materials, then it may be able to lower its cash requirements. This shows that a company that can influence accounts payable can benefit from reduced working capital.

A key objective of supply chain management, therefore, is to increase the value of DPO, for which there are two key strategies – reduce COGS or increase accounts payable. The best way of creating a virtuous circle is to focus on reducing COGS by controlling the cost of goods, materials and resources. Better management of the supply chain allows a company to reduce COGS. By contrast, supply chain glitches will have a negative impact on COGS, as we have already seen. If the cash-to-cash cycle time is still too long and a company's resources are tied up for long periods, supply chain managers, working alongside purchasing managers, should turn their efforts to adjusting the accounts payable figure by postponing payment terms to suppliers. However, it cannot be emphasized enough that this course of action should only be considered when all possible strategies for reducing COGS have already been tried.

Focusing on accounts payable is not a valid long-term strategy if suppliers suffer by being forced to wait for payment as a result of decisions taken on a unilateral basis. Longer terms of payment can be negotiated only if there is also a counter-offer that is beneficial to the supplier. Typically, this takes the form of offering the supplier a clearer view of future production volumes and/or sharing best practices to improve processes that are currently inefficient.

Accounts payable can, nevertheless, be affected by improvements in supply chain management, such as greater accuracy of forecasts and demand reliability. The study by EyeOn, cited earlier,[16] notes a potential 2 per cent reduction of purchase prices as a direct consequence of improved demand reliability. Further benefits can derive from more reliable production planning and scheduling. Clearly established parameters for materials management, such as daily delivery quantities, minimum/maximum quantities and delivery time windows, as well as agreed quality assurance protocols, are further steps that can be taken to enable a company to alter its accounts payable figure and negotiate better terms with suppliers. An enterprise must also consider the impact of education programmes that can lead to improved performance, such as lean manufacturing or Six Sigma practices.

Companies can also examine their selection of vendors in terms of tax management and foreign-exchange risks. Having multiple sources for products and having supplier contracts denominated in a range of currencies can improve financial performance. Purchasing costs can also be reduced if a company dynamically manages its allocations to suppliers in response to exchange rate shifts, giving more business to locations where the rate has depreciated and less to those facilities where the rate has appreciated.

Another important practice that can impact on the terms of purchasing contracts is the evaluation of how suppliers can effectively manage their supply chains and their ability to assume primary responsibility for product quality. The UK Office of Government Commerce, in its guide to public-sector supply chain management, urges contracting authorities to understand the importance of first-tier suppliers developing their own strong supply chain competencies for any given contract, as this will have a significant bearing on how much work the authority will need to put into influencing improvements in the performance of their supply chains:

> In many cases, a first tier supplier needs to be highly skilled in this area to deliver value for money for the contracting authority. It is also increasingly important that suppliers understand not just 'buying cheaper', but also are aware of the wider public policy considerations in procurement such as:
> - Encouraging innovation in the supply base
> - The need for openness and transparency in the entire procurement process
> - Fair and prompt payments down the supply chain.[17]

---

16 'Improved Forecast Accuracy Does Pay Back', op. cit. at fn. 9.
17 'Supply Chain Management in Public Sector Procurement', op. cit. at fn. 2.

It must be noted, however, that it could be inappropriate – and, in some cases, counterproductive – to attempt to influence suppliers in instances where supply chain management competence is not a vital ingredient in the contract. In general, the more complex the supply chain, the more important it is to try to exert some influence over first-tier suppliers with regard to how they manage those supply chains.

By now it should be clear that there are many ways in which companies can influence elements of the balance sheet and income statement reports by focusing on supply chain management. The next step is to look at how supply chain managers can find support for their attempts to positively impact on days purchasing outstanding and days sales outstanding. This support is increasingly likely to come from new entrants to the supply chain arena, namely the banks and financial services providers who are now carving out a whole new domain within the sector – the financial supply chain.

3

Managing the Flow of Goods, Information and Funds: The Role of the CFO and Financial Services Providers

We have shown that supply chain management provides the backbone for successful CRM processes, so the next logical step is to reach out to customers in a way that exploits the additional benefits that supply chain management has to offer once companies start to view it in this context. To accomplish this it is important to identify where new customers can be found and what kind of service they expect. In today's open, global and highly aggressive markets, leading companies are building their competitive edge on their supply chain management capability. At the same time, manufacturers are increasingly becoming importers, so they need to manage not only the flow of goods and information, but also – and perhaps most importantly – the flow of funds.

The strong trend among manufacturers to migrate their operations overseas and effectively become importers in order to slash their direct costs means that they have to deal with the intrinsically riskier environment of international trade. Pursuing this strategy requires investment in skills for managing long-distance supply chains. As companies increasingly operate their supply chains on a global basis to remain competitive, they also feel pressure to master unfamiliar financing tools and to operate a revised strategy for the management of working capital. The trend for companies to rapidly increase their planned direct imports and global procurement strategies has major implications for the balance sheet as they accrue in-transit inventory at some point overseas.

There is, therefore, a need to look at new ways of managing the flow of funds through the supply chain. Many of the companies that have already focused on this issue are choosing to use an open accounts structure.

The Shift to Open Accounts

With an open account, the exporter simply bills the customer, who is expected to pay under agreed terms at a future date. In a foreign transaction, this payment instrument can be a convenient method if the buyer is well established, has a long and positive payment record, or has been scrupulously checked for creditworthiness. Data-triggered finance is shifting the market towards the use of open accounts as both goods and information move ever faster through the supply chain network. However, the increasing speed at which goods and information travel is counterbalanced by the growing length of supply chains, which brings more players into the game and therefore increases fragmentation. The two major prerequisites for lean management of the supply chain – namely, trust and collaboration – become more difficult to achieve and maintain across such an extended network, so companies need to develop tools and strategies to ensure that these two factors are not compromised to the detriment of their business.

Companies at every stage of the supply chain are certainly striving to become more collaborative than ever before, as they understand the need to share forecasts and operate in a highly integrated manner. It is, after all, important that the end customer perceives the entire supply chain as fully integrated. Companies also appreciate that this objective will only be accomplished if the financial supply chain is as shared and well coordinated as the physical supply chain. It is clear, therefore, that cash flow and the management of funds are significantly more important in an environment where levels of trust are potentially lower.

New, automated solutions go some way to addressing these issues. Their goal is to significantly reduce processing costs by offering enhanced visibility and minimizing the uncertainty associated with accounts receivable and accounts payable, while also achieving a notable reduction in working capital requirement. At the same time they must also accelerate the processes of procuring goods, reconciling invoices and processing payments.

There is one major constraint that concerns supply chain professionals – how to link supply chain performance to financial decisions. As analyst Adrian Gonzalez at ARC Advisory Group points out:

> *The flow of money and the role of finance are playing a greater role in logistics and supply chain management, especially in global trade.*[1]

It is on the issue of how to manage the flow of funds that supply chain managers and chief financial officers (CFOs) come together. So far, it seems that the heavy investments in e-procurement solutions that have been made in recent years have not fed through into the correlation of payment process flows with the flows of goods and information. One typical problem is the proliferation of fragmented point solutions with very little attention paid to integration. Currently, it is still common practice to attempt rigid interorganizational integration and automation with manual processes, such as dispute resolution, reconciliation and payments. Many analysts and researchers have observed that, although the flow of information through the supply chain has accelerated, with electronic ordering now possible in seconds, and the flow of goods is faster, with many deliveries possible on the next day, the flow of funds has not kept pace. It can still take months for money to be moved along the supply chain.

An Analysis of Flows

It is possible to represent graphically the correlation between the flows of goods, information and funds, which will help not only to clarify the problems in the financial supply chain, but also to highlight potential solutions. Figure 3.1 shows how information (I), goods (G), and funds (F) interrelate as vertices – or anchor points – of a triangle.

In this diagram the arrows show how each flow correlates to the others. The name on each arrow indicates the party that 'owns' the process that links the two vertices. A simple reading of this diagram shows that the flow of information is transformed into the flow of goods and that the supply chain manager is the principal owner of the process that builds such a correlation. Supply chain managers 'own' the information in the sense that they create and control it. Through this process they are able to initiate the necessary actions and instructions to translate information into goods. The information collected

---

1   'Trends and Predictions in Transportation Systems', *Journal of Trading Partner Practices*, February–March, 2006, p. 9.

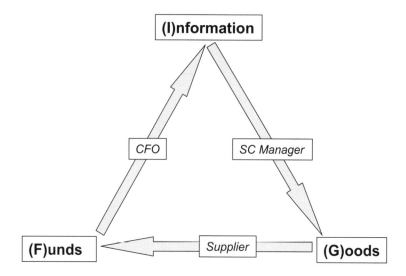

Figure 3.1   The flow of information, goods and funds

to create demand and production plans is converted into physical quantities of goods that are ordered and purchased from the supplier.

Figure 3.1 is represented as a triangle, indicating that each vertex is linked to the other two flows. The supply chain manager is able to generate new goods (represented by the arrow from I to G) by processing the data visible from the information flow – generated by forecasts, demand/production planning and sales – and the availability of funds – that is, assets and inventory. The whole purpose of managing this information depends on the supply chain manager's ability to generate value (funds) by purchasing or selling the right goods in the right quantity at the right time.

This circular relationship between the three flows can be also represented by a generic formula, which we will label (1):

$$[I] = [F] \div [G]$$

Information and goods are inversely proportional. The more information is available, the less material (that is, goods) stored in inventory is needed to create value. The reason is that stocked material offsets the lack of visibility (that is, information) of future demand.

Representing the relationship of these flows using this mathematical format helps us identify the basic components of the flows of goods and funds and generate units of measurement for both flows.

The flow of goods can be measured in terms of how much value ($) is generated per unit of quantity (q). In other words, we can investigate how much value a specific quantity of goods is able to generate, either in terms of inventory costs if we refer to raw materials, which in this case would have a negative value for the company, or in terms of sales, which would be a positive value if we consider the goods as finished products that are sold to the market.

So, we generate formula (2):

$$[G] = (\$) \div (q)$$

The way in which funds flow across the supply chain can be measured in terms of how much value ($) passes in each unit of time (t). This can be expressed as formula (3), which measures the throughput of funds over time:

$$[F] = (\$) \div (t)$$

If we put factors (2) and (3) into the original formula (1), we obtain the following equation (4):

$$[I] = [F] \div [G] = [(\$) \div (t)] \div [(\$) \div (q)] = (q) \div (t)$$

The core elements of information that supply chain managers deal with are quantity (q) and time (t). To be more precise, supply chain managers must control the information concerning what quantity (q) of goods must be ordered/managed in each time unit (t). Once again, the time factor in supply chain management comes to the fore.

If we repeat the observations above and take the same approach to analysing the flow of goods, it emerges that we can control the flow of goods once we know (that is, have sufficient information on) how much value (funds) the company wants to hold or wants to create – depending on whether we are discussing value that depends on the inventory of raw materials or on sales. Hence, formula (5):

$$[G] = [F] \div [I]$$

We already know that the units of measure for [I] are (q) and (t) as per formula [4]. For [F] it is ($) ÷ (t). Therefore, we arrive at the following equation (6):

$$[G] = [F] \div [I] = [(\$) \div (t)] \div [(q) \div (t)] = (\$) \div (q)$$

If we want to translate these numerical factors into descriptive elements, formula (6) supports the concept that the flow of goods can be measured in terms of how much value ($) is generated per unit of quantity (q) managed, whether they are raw materials or finished goods.

Finally, for the flow of funds we can derive the corresponding equation from formulas (1) and (5). From (1) we derive formula (7):

$$[F] = [I] \times [G]$$

As we have already seen – and as common practice shows us – information and goods are inversely proportional. The old adage that the purpose of supply chain management is to replace inventory (goods) with information is clearly demonstrated by this formula. A company generates the same amount of money (funds) by leveraging information and goods. The more information available, the less stocked goods, or material, are needed. It is important to understand this if we are to show the validity of the mathematical representation of the relationships between the three flows.

Formula (7) leads to formula (8):

$$[F] = [(q) \div (t)] \times [(\$) \div (q)] = (\$) \div (t).$$

Funds, therefore, flow in a way that can be measured by the value generated in a unit of time. This formula allows us to measure how much money (or cash) flows (or is needed) across the company per unit of time.

Where Do We Go From Here?

Why should it be important to consider these formulas and the relationships they represent? It should certainly be of interest for the owners of the different flows, not least because, once the units of measure for each flow have been identified, it should be easier for them to focus on the key levers that enable them to improve the management of those flows.

It follows from this analysis that we should focus more precisely on who the owners of the various flows are. We have already identified the supply chain manager as the owner of the information flow, and the fact that $[I] = (q) \div (t)$ suggests that the time unit is the key item on which the supply chain manager should concentrate. This enables better decisions to be made about the quantity of goods a company is capable of issuing per unit of time. Using the terminology of the Theory of Constraints, as outlined in *The Goal* by the theory's originator Eli Goldratt[2], this is what we will call 'throughput'. Once we attach a price-tag to a quantity of goods shipped we derive a company's sales figure. This then translates into how much revenue the company is able to produce per unit of time. Although we say 'revenue', everyone would agree that what really counts is profit. Given that profit is calculated once price and costs are known, we must now identify the source of costs, which will help us elaborate on the equation.

The Sources of Cost

When a significant portion of overall cost is determined by the cost of materials, the sourced quantities from suppliers should, as far as possible, be aligned with the number of units requested by the supply chain per unit of time. Here the velocity of goods – the time factor – becomes less important than the cost attached to each unit.

To the supply chain manager the cost per unit is the cost paid by the buyer as part of the overall buyer–vendor relationship. At the other end of the chain we have the vendor – or supplier – who looks at the same equation but replaces 'cost' with 'value'. What is seen as cost for the buyer becomes the price value for the supplier. The value per unit of quantity, therefore, becomes the unit of measurement when managing the flow of goods. This we represent in formula (6):

$$[G] = (\$) \div (q)$$

So, we must now identify who 'owns' these goods. The answer sits on the arrow in Figure 3.1 that moves from goods to funds – the supplier. Following the logic of the model that sees each vertex firmly linked to the other two, we

2   E.M. Goldratt and J. Cox, *The Goal: A Process of Ongoing Improvement*, Great Barrington, MA: North River Press, 1984.

learn that suppliers perform best when they are able to get the most value [F] from each unit of information exchanged with the supply chain manager of the buying company. We know this from formula (5):

$$[G] = [F] \div [I]$$

From formula (6) we see that the time factor, which is of such vital importance to the management of information by the supply chain manager, is subsumed by the quantity factor (q). The supplier of goods must focus on delivering quantity to get value. If the supplier delivers on time but in the wrong quantity, it is penalized in the form of delayed or reduced payments (F).

If we read (5) and (6) together, we can conclude from the model that, by focusing on the value ($) generated by selling a unit of goods (q), the supplier generates funds [F] – represented in Figure 3.1 by the arrow from goods to funds – by delivering the right goods according to the information it has received – that is, customer demand, forecasts and inventory.

As we have already seen, the third vertex of the model is represented by formula (7):

$$[F] = [I] \times [G].$$

The model tells us that it is the CFO who 'owns' the flow of funds. Through these funds, as well as the visibility of goods – such as the three-way matching of invoice, purchase order and proof of delivery – the CFO generates information, as indicated by the direction of the arrow from (F) to (I). In other words, the CFO provides the visibility of company results. This information can be identified with the budget targets set by the finance department for the operations team, such as inventory levels, working capital requirements and cash flow objectives. It is the same information that the supply chain manager needs to know in order to initiate another iteration of the [I] → [G] → [F] cycle.

From Models to Reality

Of course, no model as simple as that described in Figure 3.1 can be said to encapsulate all of the subtleties of the real world of business. In fact, the model is distorted in the real world by various 'attractors', which divert the linear flows that make up its neat triangular shape. These additional players in the cycle expand

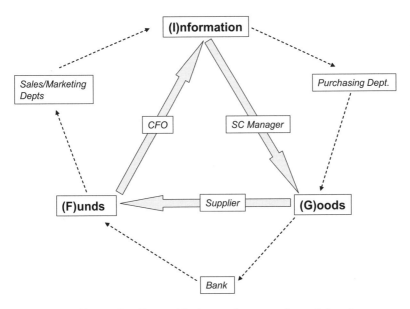

Figure 3.2   Pulls on the flow of information, goods and funds

the closed $[I] \rightarrow [G] \rightarrow [F]$ loop, as shown in Figure 3.2, the obvious result being an increase in the time it takes to flow from one vertex to another. Yet again, we see the importance of the time factor in the management of the supply chain.

The first 'pull' to notice is that exerted by sales and marketing on the (F) $\rightarrow$ (I) flow, which increases the time funds take to generate information. While this transition should seamlessly represent the means by which supply chain managers obtain indications of the budgeted inventory levels around which they must establish the policies and strategies of their operations, new functional roles – sales and marketing – inject additional elements that distort the linear flow. Sales and discount policies, new product launches and promotional campaigns are all attractors, which bend the linear trajectory of the (F) $\rightarrow$ (I) flow.

The unit of measure that gauges the performance of this attractor is derived from the combination of formulas (8) and (4):

$$[F] \rightarrow [I] = [(\$) \div (t)] \rightarrow [(q) \div (t)]$$

Hence, the unit of measure of the sales/marketing attractor is formula (9):

$$(q) \div (\$)$$

$$[(\$) \div (t) \times (q) \div (\$)] \rightarrow (q) \div (t)$$

This equation effectively models the behaviour of these functional departments, the focus of which is to maximize the quantity a company can deliver per unit of value – in other words, to show the customer that he gets the most out of the value he has paid for. Formula (9) also captures the effect of a promotional marketing campaign – that is, to offer the highest quantity possible (q) for the least money paid ($).

Given that sales and marketing engage with clients and prospects to achieve the maximum value per unit of product that the company can deliver, this would be better expressed by the ($) ÷ (q) unit of measurement. Why, therefore, does the model instead use the inverse calculation for the sales/marketing attractor?

An attractor is defined as a factor that bends and distorts the linear flow from one vertex to the other. It therefore creates disturbance in the normal flow. What actually happens is that sales and marketing on one side tend to put pressure on the supply chain, so that what has been promised – the quantity (q) already virtually sold and therefore the source of value ($) – gets delivered as soon as possible.

The (q) ÷ ($) formula exactly models this phenomenon – now that the company has generated value ($) from sales, it must make sure that it supplies the whole maximum quantity (q) against that value. To be more precise, the 'whole maximum quantity (q)' should be read as 'the whole quantity (q) promised to the client to arrive at the right time', which again shows clearly that the time factor is tightly linked to the performance of the supply chain manager.

The attractor affecting the [I] → [G] flow is purchasing. Bending the flow from [I] to [G] means moving from the (q) ÷ (t) unit of measure to ($) ÷ (q), so the distorting factor is one that converts (q) ÷ (t) into ($) ÷ (q). By quick calculation we can conclude that the unit of measurement for the purchasing attractor is $(\$ \times t) \div (q)^2$.

Even though this formula might appear complicated and its explanation too stretched, the conclusions are nevertheless realistic and the model still holds true. To explain $(\$ \times t) \div (q)^2$ we can decompose it into formula (10):

$$[(\$) \div (q)] \times [(t) \div (q)]$$

The ($) ÷ (q) factor measures the distorting effect of the purchasing function when it focuses its efforts on minimizing the price ($) paid per unit of quantity purchased (q) or, to put it another way, reducing the purchasing price for the same amount of goods purchased.

The (t) ÷ (q) component takes into account the purchasing function's additional distorting effect on the normal course of the relationship between supply chain and supplier when the focus is on the delivery time of the goods purchased. Every supply chain manager knows that the time factor is important, but equally important is the fact that it must not generate any disruptive effects by putting continuous pressure on the supplier. A better delivery performance – (t) ÷ (q), the time it takes to deliver the unit of quantity (must be achieved through better management and exchange of information – better forecasts and improved visibility of inventory) and information is not only the anchor point of Figure 3.1, but is also directly under the supply chain manager's supervision and control.

Figure 3.2 shows that banks play the role of attractor in the (G) → (F) flow, a fact that can easily be observed in a company's day-to-day business. Suppliers ship goods with the aim of maximizing the value received per unit of quantity delivered ($ ÷ q). The buyer's finance department looks at how to manage its working capital more effectively by maximizing the value ($) per unit of time (t), as represented in formula (8) in the model: ($ ÷ t).

Banks are assuming the key role of intermediaries in modern supply chains, providing buyer, and supplier, with financing in order to reduce their clients' financial risk when dealing with remote partners, and to help them take advantage of the cost of capital structures in different regions around the world. There will be a more detailed description of the role of banks later, but for now it is important to understand how banks create a distorting effect in the linear flow between goods and funds.

The shift from (G) to (F) transforms the unit of measure from ($ ÷ q) to ($ ÷ t). The unit of measurement that gauges the effect of the bank attractor is, therefore, (q ÷ t). In analytical terms, this measures the quantity of goods that are in transit per unit of time under the control of the bank.

The validity of this representation becomes evident when flows of funds are blocked because documents are not well drafted or when there has been a failure to comply with regulations, in which case the bank is prevented from clearing the transaction and cannot make the goods physically available to the buyer. The need to create and manage financial and trade documents is particularly crucial in the use of letters of credit (LCs), which will be discussed in more detail later. For now, it is sufficient to know that the physical flow of goods can be blocked or hindered by the lack of proper documentation accompanying the trade.

For that reason, the structure of supply chain trade finance is moving away from documentation such as LCs which are increasingly giving way to open accounts. In an open account structure, both importer and exporter sign a contract stating that the importer will send the exporter the required funds for the goods at some point in the future.

The direct consequence of this shift in market trends is that supply chain management capabilities must be enriched with document and compliance management processes that reflect global trade practices. Without a proper understanding of trade regulations or the ability to create and process documentation accurately a company risks higher landed costs, regulatory penalties, higher duty payments, longer cash-to-cash cycles, charges for discrepancies in LCs and additional costs from delays in clearing customs.

Unlike domestic trade, where normal practice is to send electronic purchase orders and receive electronic shipping notices and invoices, in the world of global trade there are many more points at which timing problems can arise once a product has been ordered. Any new strategy that takes a company into the arena of global trade must evolve from the traditional practice of merely optimizing the physical logistics capability of its supply chain to addressing the dislocation of distribution centres, allocation of stocks, selection of carriers and production outsourcing decisions.

We need to ask, therefore, what it means to design and plan a supply chain from both physical and financial perspectives. How can the supply chain manager, in close collaboration with the CFO, establish a correct balance between the two?

A manufacturer relies on a bank or finance company to provide capital for purchasing raw materials, financing inventories and discounting receivables. Working capital is the key indicator that measures the integration of the flow of goods (supply chain management) and the flow of funds (financial supply chain). The models of the financial supply chain currently available represent financial supply chain solutions purely in terms of how supply chain management processes correspond to financial transactions, such as the sourcing of goods with accounts payable, manufacturing with working capital, and the shipping of goods with accounts receivable. These models that map financial transactions against supply chain processes suggest that the two are still separate domains with flows that move in tandem, yet never really become intertwined. This is because supply chain processes are used to represent the flow of goods and information, while the financial supply chain represents the flow of funds.

It might, for example, be asked whether an individual working in the field of operations and who is thus concerned with the supply chain would know exactly which processes in the financial flow are triggered when a purchase order is issued. Would that individual know what happens in the accounting books and general ledger when goods are received in the warehouse, or when an item is rejected because of poor quality?

The bottom line is that the supply chain transaction is not completed until the invoice is paid and taxes are recovered. All the good work put into planning can be for nothing if the transaction fails. A supply chain will not be truly optimized so long as the flow of funds requires months of reconciliations and clearances, even if electronic ordering takes only a few seconds and goods are delivered the next day. This is what the model described in Figure 3.2 attempts to explain by featuring the bank attractor and the (q ÷ t) unit of measure.

The Role of the CFO

The role of the chief financial officer within a company has evolved significantly in recent years and has been especially affected by the development of supply chain management. The Supply Chain recently conducted a survey among supply chain managers and financial directors to evaluate the level of maturity of the supply chain function in numerous companies and to determine how well it has been aligned with other corporate functions.[3] The survey also strove to verify whether the alignment of supply chain and finance functions has led to greater consensus between these disciplines on performance measures and the perceived correlation between operational and financial metrics.

---

3   E. Camerinelli, 'Measuring the Value of the Supply Chain: Linking Financial Decisions with Supply Chain Performance', available at: http://www.supply-chain.org/galleries/public-gallery/Measuring%20the%20Value%20of%20the%20SCpromo.pdf.

The Supply Chain Council based the survey on a number of external interviews with supply chain executives from organizations including Borealis Group, Heineken, Holcim, Siemens, Innersoft and Reckitt Benckiser. The majority of interviewees were in middle-management roles or at higher levels such as vice presidents of procurement or supply chain management corporate process executives. Most of the companies chosen for the survey were keen to improve their processes, their operations and the linkages between operational metrics and financial performance. Furthermore, they were all manufacturing companies, though from a range of different industries, whose supply chain accounted for a considerable proportion of their operations.

The telephone interviews that formed part of the survey covered a range of topics, including: the level of agreement among functions such as finance and logistics regarding performance measures; the strength of the linkages between supply chain and finance; the economic impact of supply chain decisions; where within the organization the responsibility lies for setting and monitoring supply chain targets; and the reward systems in place for supply chain executives.

Whether or not comprehensive supply chain measurement systems are used depends heavily on board-level perception of the supply chain function and, so far, there has been very little academic research into this subject. A study carried out by Gooch and Menachof [4] examined the differences in perception between board members and supply chain executives to identify how they could be resolved. The results indicate that the supply chain function is generally appreciated as an important factor in achieving sustainable competitive advantage. Some 60 per cent of respondents believed knowledge of supply chain issues at board level to be 'Good', while 56 per cent stated that they felt the supply chain function had a significant impact on a company's economic performance.

In most circumstances it is managing directors, vice presidents, financial directors and members of the board of directors who define the objectives of the supply chain, and the survey highlighted their main objectives when doing so:

- profit/cost control (31 per cent)

- supplier and contract responsibilities (31 per cent)

- stock control/inventory management (21 per cent).

---

4   S. Gooch and D. Menachof, *Board Perception of the Supply Chain Function*, London: Cass Business School, 2003.

In contrast, the responsibilities identified by supply chain managers are much more specific:

- delivery and service level provision (35 per cent)

- cost control and product pricing (29 per cent)

- stock control/inventory management (25 per cent)

- forecasting (11 per cent).

The Supply Chain Council survey also highlighted that the lack of a clear understanding of supply chain management in some company departments such as sales and marketing can create conflict between the objectives these functions set and the goals of supply chain professionals. As a result, supply chain managers are often forced to share decisions with managers of other departments, which may result in them being confined to a routine series of operational supervision tasks. To remedy this situation, supply chain managers must learn to communicate the results of their work in financial language that can be better understood by other departments.

CFOs are concerned with cash-to-cash cycle time, working capital and cash flow from operations. By contrast, supply chain managers are concerned with issues such as the reliability of forecasts, inventory returns and on-time delivery. One reason why the finance function does not use operational metrics is that they do not fit well with the language normally used in accounting and finance processes. The challenge, therefore, is to effectively translate the results from operations into financial measures.

A Big Gap to Bridge

Respondents had fairly similar views on all the topics that fell within the scope of the Supply Chain Council survey.[5] For instance, on the matter of whether the finance function and supply chain executives agree on performance measures all except one respondent said there is no agreement.

There are many reasons why this is so. First, there are difficulties in translating qualitative (that is, 'soft' or 'intangible') measures – such as

---

5   Camerinelli, 'Measuring the Value of the Supply Chain', op. cit. at fn. 3.

metrics on reliability, responsiveness and flexibility – into financial indicators. Second, there is no unique set of metrics or single measurement to monitor the performance and efficiency of the supply chain. Third, there is a lack of common definitions for metrics and for coordination between the two functions.

All the respondents stated that there are some signs in their organizations that the links between their supply chains and finance functions are becoming stronger. For instance, in some organizations supply chain metrics are included in their main and mandatory corporate targets. However, some issues have been identified as causes of inefficiency. These include the lack of a common language shared by supply chain managers and CFOs, the lack of a comprehensive framework, including financial metrics and supply chain aggregate measures, and contradictory goals set by different departments.

All the respondents concurred that they now recognize the economic impact of supply chain decisions and, furthermore, they believed that the supply chain is now perceived as a strategic element in the pursuit of competitive advantage. Nevertheless, some organizations still tend to focus simply on cutting costs in the supply chain rather than using it to generate value.

Regarding the level at which supply chain targets are defined, this seems to vary from company to company. In most cases, high-level metrics are set at corporate level while operational metrics are set and monitored at functional level. Supply chain targets are increasingly set at corporate level, translated into financial goals by chief financial officers and cascaded down. This approach – top-down versus bottom-up – seems to indicate that the supply chain has greater visibility at board level.

In some cases, the survey's respondents perceive many reasons for the difficulties in setting and monitoring operational targets at functional level. These include:

- lack of guidelines at corporate level

- lack of a common language with which to communicate supply chain measures to the CFO or the board

- lack of proven links between certain supply chain metrics, such as flexibility, and financial measures

- difficulties associated with incorporating uncertainty and risk into targets

- lack of standard metrics

- lack of supply chain representation at board level, resulting in the board failing to appreciate the trade-offs involved in supply chain decisions.

There are also discrepancies between companies in respect of the supply chain executives' reward systems and incentives. Generally, their incentives are linked to both financial and operational targets. However, from middle management downwards, rewards seem to be linked either to solely operational metrics or partly to customer service levels – that is, based on factors such as product availability, pack fill rate or order fill rate – and partly to financial performance, where factors such as networking capital have an impact.

The Supply Chain Council survey's respondents acknowledged the pressing need for a framework correlating supply chain measures with financial performance that could facilitate better communication between supply chain managers and CFOs. In short, they recognize the need to translate the effectiveness of supply chain management into monetary terms and reflect these data in an organization's financial statements.

The Next Stage of Evolution for CFOs

To assess the relevance of the financial officer in the overall ecosystem of supply chain management we need to look at the pressures and trends in the officer's role and reach.

In the light of the survey results it emerges that supply chain managers need to take a new stance in relation to the CFO. They must become more like advisers, counsellors or coaches instead of remaining as cost-accounting gatekeepers and pass/fail rulers of budget proposals. The role of the CFO is also changing in the light of the pressure of market dynamics and newly emerging industry trends. The finance function must have a holistic and horizontal view of the enterprise, but to maintain this it must know precisely where the enterprise is and where it is headed. This kind of control is achieved through data and, if data are largely collected manually, the principal role of the finance department is that of controller and gatekeeper, ensuring that procedures are properly executed. Little time is left to perform more value-adding activities.

As levels of automation increase, systems become better integrated – which is why finance is often in control of IT – and there is more empowerment of both people and functions within the organization. The finance department then has more time to play the role of counsellor and provider of knowledge to other corporate functions. Standardization of processes enables the handover of accountability in a controlled fashion, as is highlighted in research by IBM, which states:

> In the past, practical limitations forced Finance organizations to focus primarily on only one of these [corporate] focus areas (for example, performance, growth or risk), but process and technology improvements make it possible to do more. Indeed, by applying financial management discipline to the enterprise-wide delivery of predictive business insight, CFOs seek to strengthen their roles as trusted advisers and become true business partners with their CEOs and business unit leaders.[6]

The transition to this more high-tech environment is far from complete. In fact, IBM's research suggests that finance organizations are often still struggling to standardize and improve processes and data structures and to implement the technology that underpins enhanced decision support. The study further warns that, if common processes and standards are not adopted across an enterprise, then intuition alone becomes the main tool for financial management and an organization may find itself exposed to greater risk by relying solely on the manual effort of a small number of smart individuals to maintain the accuracy and integrity of its financial information. The study notes that:

> This reliance embeds unique knowledge in individuals versus institutionalizing it into repeatable, controlled processes and technology that can be shared more widely ... Without a strategy to mitigate structural complexity and a strictly enforced adherence policy, Finance will struggle constantly to provide insights, primarily relying on time-consuming manual consolidation of static spreadsheets. A common result is time wasted discussing the veracity of the data instead of focusing on the information provided and analysing it to provide predictive insights ... Not surprisingly, process simplification

---

6   IBM Business Consulting Services, *The Agile CFO: Acting on Business Insight, IBM*, 2005, p. 7 available at: http://www-935.ibm.com/services/us/imc/pdf/ge510-6239-agile-cfo-full.pdf.

also helps drive integration. With less to consolidate and information captured at the source, it becomes easier to integrate the information and processes to provide key insights.[7]

In a more streamlined and highly automated environment CFOs can look beyond their traditional role as guardians of the accuracy and transparency of financial statements. The control and compliance functions for which they are responsible become more standardized tasks, reliant on embedded alerts, dashboard analytics and workflow systems. When risk analysis is embedded in the day-to-day routine of managing a business, CFOs can be more proactive, focusing more on governance and planning as opposed to data collection and reporting.

Tomorrow's successful CFOs will spend more time and energy building insight capabilities across all departments within their organizations in a bid to achieve the agility they need to respond quickly to changes in their business environment. This is why many finance departments are making greater efforts to map processes and clarify the structure of process ownership, taking responsibility for key data away from separate business units and recognizing those data as corporate assets that can deliver value throughout the enterprise.

This will profoundly change the CFO's role. Responsibility for data accuracy will remain with the source of the data, but finance will become accountable for its overall integrity. The CFO, therefore, has complete control over corporate assets and information.

This new definition of the role that CFOs play within an organization lays the foundation for them to better understand and to engage more fully with the supply chain. To do so, they need a clear set of metrics and a shared language through which the two disciplines can interact in a more meaningful way. Indeed, CFOs need to improve communication with all parts of their enterprises.

Managers of individual business units now expect CFOs to become highly adept at gathering, interpreting and distributing information – both financial and non-financial – across an organization. The finance function must be in a position to explain any problems that arise and to take a proactive approach to solving those problems before they spiral out of control. Finance will play an increasingly important part in alerting managers of various business lines

---

7   Ibid., pp. 10, 13 and 14.

to potential pitfalls and helping them gear up for forthcoming challenges. To achieve this, CFOs will be more reliant on technology. Many business-critical IT systems have their roots in the finance function, often stemming from internal transaction and data processing needs. It seems, therefore, that CFOs will also need to take more responsibility for their organizations' key systems.

Technology and the CFO

The widespread implementation of business performance management in the day-to-day operations of many companies is one example of a system that falls under the CFO's control. It demonstrates that the finance function is expected to manage a growing amount of non-financial data, which is then used to influence decisions that affect every area of a business. The goal is to increase the use of ERP systems and analytical tools in order to achieve more detailed analysis and predictive modelling, on the basis of which strategic decisions will be made. This pursuit of enhanced performance management frameworks inevitably leads to a cascading of metrics down to all business units and all functions. Currently, however, there has been slower progress in delivering these metrics than there has been with the development and implementation of executive scorecards, and this gap needs to be bridged.

Traditionally, the responsibilities of CFOs have centred on issues of control and treasury, with tasks like budgeting at their core. Today, CFOs must ensure not only that the most appropriate IT systems are in place to measure corporate and departmental goals, but also that these systems enable them to move the organization towards attaining these goals. What today's CFOs are trying to achieve is enhanced insight across their entire organizations, which they hope will deliver greater agility and, consequently, increased profitability in rapidly evolving markets. Those who achieve the best results do so by defining quantifiable relationships between the drivers of their business and the metrics used in executive scorecards and dashboards, which enable them to improve the effectiveness and accuracy of their predictive analysis and performance outcome forecasts. Their most important goals are to manage enterprise performance more efficiently, foster growth by partnering with all of the elements of their enterprise, improve their organization's business processes and ensure that they meet their regulatory and fiduciary requirements. Central to achieving these goals is the ability to work more closely and effectively with senior management, including the CEO and the leaders of individual business units, to ensure that all possible synergies are identified and all opportunities for performance improvement are acted upon.

CFOs still need to remain focused on the important financial controls, such as effective cash flow and expenses management, customer credit policies for customers, establishing favourable payment terms with important vendors and optimizing the measurement and management of inventory levels. They will also need to handle projects where significant quantitative and qualitative analysis is required if they are to have a clear view of all their options. In developing an annual budget, for instance, finance officers will need to communicate with all department managers within their organization to ensure that their budgets are accurate, in line with strategic goals and reflect the true state of the business. Vital to this is their ability to implement effective means for ongoing communication with all sources of financial data. They must, therefore, develop strong working relationships with financial institutions, which may significantly influence an enterprise's capacity to finance its operations. As one CFO says:

> A crucial aspect of [treasury] activity involves ongoing communication with these financial sources. Investors and debt holders must be kept apprized of the goals and performance of the company, in order to keep these channels open. They must understand how the pursuit of these goals impacts the risks and returns on their investments. An uninformed investment community will not be a ready source of funds.[8]

Bringing together information from all internal departments and external providers of financial services enables CFOs to offer vital insight to CEOs about the financial resources their companies will need in order to achieve their strategic goals. They provide a vital bridge between banks, business units and the board, thanks to the detailed and sensitive information and analysis they coordinate. Successful financial managers will play a vital part in keeping senior executives informed and in guiding their businesses, provided that they can make a strong and tangible connection between operations and financial performance, and couple this with their own business acumen and finance skills.

The Role of Banks

Modern supply chains are greatly extending their reach and, as a result, the distance between suppliers, manufacturers and customers is growing larger. Geographical distance, however, is not the only factor to consider. We must

---

8   Ken Colabella, 'The Role of the CFO', 24 January 2006, at: http://www.colabella.net/index. php?option=com_content&task=view&id=26&Itemid=40&PHPSESSID=3f143b26175ba1b34e2c 047833ad4279.

also look at the process management distance and the regulatory and financial distance to gauge the separation between the many constituents in the supply chain.

The importance of visibility in managing the supply chain should already be clear in all its aspects – products, processes, partners and profit. The last two visibility factors, partners and profit, are of particular importance, especially when cultural differences increasingly affect newly formed business relationships. The way in which business is managed in the Far East compares only loosely to the way in which Western companies approach such matters. While US and Western European companies strive to automate production processes to reduce cost and increase efficiency, manufacturing companies in low-cost emerging countries (for example, China and its neighbours) still tend to prefer manual-intensive operations.

Cultural differences in those regions arise not only in the selection of new suppliers, where local contacts and family-based relationships replace normal entrepreneurial business relationships, but also in closing business deals, which may often involve seemingly interminable negotiations. Furthermore, almost any import transaction involving the Far East requires a letter of credit as the customary instrument to secure execution of a deal. The role of banks and other financial institutions in delivering visibility and efficiency in the supply chain, therefore, becomes crucial as geographical, process and financial distances increase.

In today's new supply chain economy a bank must represent a trusted party that offers cost-effective access to an extensive geographical network and a comprehensive service to support the timely flow of accurate payments between all players along the supply chain. As part of this service they must pay attention to the working capital requirements of overseas suppliers, not just of importers. Working capital finance helps smaller exporters buy materials or fabricate their products.

Currently, letters of credit are the primary tools for the management of financial flows associated with bringing in inventory from overseas. The letter of credit is a document issued by a bank at the request of the importer, whereby the bank agrees to accept and/or pay drafts drawn upon it by the exporter. Suppliers in Taiwan, Hong Kong or Thailand, for example, present the letter to their local bank, which uses it as the basis for lending pre-shipment working capital. In the past few years, however, both banks and non-bank financial services organizations have been working to expand the range of options for importers and, in doing so, have been looking for a much more innovative way of getting back into financing trade. The big banks, such as J.P. Morgan Chase and Wells Fargo HSBC Trade Bank which run huge processing centres in Hong Kong and neighbouring countries, are moving to a new strategy: their electronic systems automatically convert purchase orders to letters of credit or open accounts, while they use their presence on the ground in East Asia to finance the local suppliers. Then there are entities such as UPS, the transport-logistics player, which is becoming increasingly visible in trade finance. Its finance arm, UPS Capital, bought a bank in 2002, issues its own letters of credit, and merges the physical and financial supply chains.

Letters of Credit

As stated above, the letter of credit is the preferred financial instrument in the majority of import–export deals involving companies in the Far East, and the industry in general is still very cautious about changing its habits to favour other solutions that do not guarantee the same reduction of financial risk. The processes behind the issuance of letters of credit involve rigorous control and securitization of all parties and funds involved. At the same time, however, the costs incurred in managing these instruments of credit are extremely high, largely because they involve manual-intensive, paper-based processes.

When an overseas buyer approaches its bank to issue a letter of credit to the exporter's bank, both buyer and bank are formalizing a promise to pay that exporter for its goods. The exporter, however, must comply with all of the letter's terms and conditions. Payment is not based on terms of sale or physical condition of the goods, but instead on documentation. The letter of credit specifies that the exporter present certain documents such as an ocean bill of lading, consular invoice, draft and insurance policy. It also has an expiry date. The bank that will be responsible for making payment first verifies that all the required documentation is presented in line with the letter of credit's specifications. Any discrepancies in the documentation must be resolved before the expiry date if payment is to be successfully made.

In addition, exporters have an opportunity to confirm a letter of credit issued by foreign banks if they are not familiar with that bank or if they have concerns about risks – political or economic – in the country where that bank is located. They may call upon international banks or export assistance centres, for example, to help them assess such risks in order to clarify what processes and safeguards may be appropriate in any specific export transaction.

We can clearly see, therefore, that many steps are required for the issuance of a letter of credit. Typically, a letter confirmed by a European bank goes through the following stages:

- Following agreement of the sales terms, the buyer instructs its bank to prepare a letter of credit, specifying the required documentation.

- The bank issues a letter of credit, and instructions for the shipment are relayed to the seller.

- The letter of credit is sent to a European bank with a request for confirmation.

- The European bank drafts a confirmation letter that is sent to the exporter with an irrevocable letter of credit.

- The exporter reviews the conditions of the letter and negotiates with its freight partner to ensure that the specified shipping date can be met.

- Any concerns about the exporter's ability to comply with the letter of credit's conditions are communicated to the buyer.

- The exporter arranges the delivery of goods to a specified place where the freight partner can take possession of them.

- The goods are loaded for shipment, and the freight company completes a further set of documents.

- The documentation is presented to the European bank to ensure compliance with the letter of credit's terms.

- The bank verifies the documentation and, provided that it is in order, sends it to the buyer's bank and, subsequently, to the buyer for review.

- The buyer uses the documents to claim the goods.

- The buyer's bank pays the draft sent with the letter of credit to the exporter's bank at the agreed time.

The stages listed above may vary, as indeed may the costs involved. Banks charge different rates for issuing letters of credit, depending on the type of relationship a company has with its bank, the term of the letter, the amount of funds represented by the letter of credit and many other factors. In many cases, exporters do not understand the full extent of the credit implications and costs that face buyers using these letters as instruments for credit. For example, to get a letter of credit a buyer must arrange an appropriate credit facility with the issuing bank. Costs certainly vary, depending on where the buyer is located and which bank it uses, but in the developed world it can be assumed as a guideline that obtaining a letter of credit may incur a cost of up to 4 per cent if the letter's value exceeds $100 000, while elsewhere in the world the cost can still be 1.5 per cent or more. In addition to these costs, buyers have to consider the implications of the many manual operations involved in the process, as well as the statistical evidence which indicates that the seller's documentation is rejected by banks in as much as 50 per cent of letter-of-credit transactions.

Seeking Alternatives to Letters of Credit

Those enterprises that are deeply involved in supply chain import–export trade are constantly looking for solutions that mitigate the costs associated with manual-intensive operations. These solutions must, however, ensure the same level of risk avoidance that makes the letter of credit so popular. These organizations are understandably looking to banks to provide alternative solutions.

Current initiatives among banks are focused on two strands of development. First, standards for technology frameworks such as SWIFTNet and electronic invoice presentation and payment (EIPP) are evolving. Second, there are moves to improve trade exchange interoperability, with initiatives such as the Single Euro Payments Area (SEPA).

The combination of electronic information flows and the security of working on both ends of a transaction – with buyer and seller – creates an environment that significantly mitigates risk. The initial approach of looking for a technical

solution through a common meta-format for payment settlements has proven
to be the wrong one, as have attempts to replace good business practices in
process analysis and revision with the simple purchase of technology, which
has been the cause of seemingly endless debate for many years. The senior cash
management specialist at a large bank has neatly observed:

> *The first, simpler and more inevitable step in the payment chain, namely
> offering a standardised, fail-safe transfer channel independent of banks,
> was neglected. … Banks have invested large amounts in the ongoing
> development of better electronic banking products, and then used these
> projects to set themselves apart from their competitors.*[9]

When examined more closely, however, electronic banking software is
merely an interface to close the integration gap between credit/debit payment
streams within the company and within a bank's processes. It is not a decisive
customer link.

Financial services providers have now learnt that lesson and are focusing
on their core competencies and objectives that may deliver competitive
advantage – namely, efficiency, speed of payments processing, the
transmission of information and the quality of advice they can offer. This
approach is extremely valuable to finance executives who are personally
liable for compliance in the wake of regulations such as the International
Financial Reporting Standards (IFRS) and the Sarbanes-Oxley Act of
2002. The IFRS prescribe rules and guidelines to achieve one global set of
accounting standards. The CFO Executive Board blog[10] reminds us that
foreign subsidiaries of many US companies operating in nations which have
adopted IFRS usually prepare financial statements in both IFRS and US GAAP.
Subsidiaries are required to prepare IFRS-based financial statements as per
standard reporting requirements in the country of operation, and prepare
financial statements using US GAAP to facilitate the consolidation of group
profits. The immediate consequence is that financial officers of US companies
with major competitors operating in nations which have adopted IFRS must
resist comparing financial parameters with their competitors because of the
underlying differences between the two accounting systems. Sarbanes-Oxley
is a US federal law enacted in response to a number of major corporate and
accounting scandals including those affecting Enron, Tyco International,
Peregrine Systems and WorldCom, which resulted in a decline of public trust

---

9   J. Lutz, HVB, April 2006, at: http:// www.gtnews.com/article/6322.cfm.
10 At: http://www.cfo.exbdblog.com.

in accounting and reporting practices. The law requires senior executives of all US public company boards, management and public accounting firms – including all subsidiaries – to certify the truthfulness of their corporations' reports, under the penalty of imprisonment and the payment of hefty fines.

As a result, finance directors now pay more attention to decentralizing their companies' payment activities. The downside of this strategy is that, because there are a large number of processes to analyse and software products to adopt, making the auditing process expensive and time-consuming, the efforts to comply with these regulations are generating a strong impulse towards greater standardization and centralization of payment processes.

The next step for the major trade banks is to further reduce the gap between the global supply chain and the finance chain by adopting more common standards for electronic documents and their transfer. Information is now the common ingredient among the movers of goods and movers of money.

Banks are trying to narrow the gap on several fronts. One example is SWIFTNet. Large international banks – including significant European players such as ABN AMRO, BNP Paribas, Deutsche Bank, The Royal Bank of Scotland and San Paolo IMI – have recently signed an agreement to pilot the SWIFTNet Trade Services Utility (TSU) solution, a central matching and workflow engine that uses industry standards, and the SWIFTNet messaging network to enable banks to provide new and enhanced services in supply chain management. Further examples include EIPP and other Internet-based electronic invoicing solutions. The ultimate goal of organizations that have made the move to electronic management of some of their transactions is to achieve automated processing. The most significant business challenges associated with the invoice-to-payment cycle enabled through electronic transactions typically centre on reducing the volume of physical paper transactions, particularly the wide use of cheque payments and the continued use of paper invoices.

Companies will benefit most from an end-to-end solution that automates the entire transaction process for both buyer and seller. Ideally, this would cover electronic delivery of a purchase order for online supplier review and approval, submission of supplier documents, invoice comparison, electronic discrepancy reports, images of documents related to the transaction, all the way to reconciliation and payment. This is the so-called open accounts mechanism.

Although open accounts eliminate the processing and service fees incurred when traditional trade instruments are used, they do present an administrative burden. Companies must take on the document processing activities previously handled by banks where letters of credit were used. For many companies, this entails consolidating data from multiple sources and matching commercial invoices or bills of lading with purchase orders. This manual process is both time-consuming and subject to error. Technology can enhance this process and remove the documentation risk by ensuring that the invoice conforms to the purchase order. However, commonly agreed standard procedures between trading partners must be established before this automation can occur. Nevertheless, many organizations are keen to take this step and agree on the required standards. The Association for Financial Professionals provides professional certification, continuing education, public policy research, development of industry standards, financial tools and publications, training and career development, and representation to legislators and regulators. In a survey run by the Association[11] 78 per cent of respondents said they were either 'very likely' or 'somewhat likely' to make the transition from paper cheques to electronic payments for their business-to-business payments by 2008. This behaviour has been confirmed by anecdotal experience.

On a less technology-oriented front there is the SEPA initiative, which originated from the EU's Lisbon Conference, where the idea emerged of supporting innovation and the single market by making it simpler and cheaper to move money around the European Union. The fundamental concept of SEPA is that cross-border money transfers in the Euro Zone should cost no more than domestic transfers, and the group of banks constituting the European Payments Council has sketched out plans for how this will be become a reality by 2010. However, for it to be successful banks will have to sharpen up their IT systems to automate manual processes if they are to bring down costs.

Despite these various initiatives, supply chain managers still have no indication of what or how information should be prepared when planning the supply chain in order to ensure that supply chain management processes (flows of goods and information) interlock with financial processes (flows of information and funds).

A supply chain manager's plan should provide benefit to the entire automated outsourcing process – for goods, information and funds – on both

---

11 Association of Financial Professionals, 'Payments Risk Survey, Report of Survey Results' March 2006 at: http://www.afponline.org/pub/pdf/PaymentsRiskSurvey_1.pdf.

buyer and seller sides of a transaction. This would cover all the elements of the open accounts mechanism. Supply chain planning must factor in financial processes within the expected electronic transactions.

Up until now, the financial transactions of an ERP system have translated into accounts receivable, accounts payable, cash flows and events at the physical level. They can be envisioned as an *ex-post* mapping. This immediately raises the following questions:

- What should the supply chain manager do before he plans for the material and information process flows, in order to take into account the correlated financial process flows in an *ex-ante* mode?

- What data needs to be prepared to interconnect and correlate the material, information and financial flows?

- At what step in the process should this preparation of information take place?

- Are there any industry standard best practices for this?

BANKS SENSE A BUSINESS OPPORTUNITY

Answering these questions demands a shift to a new paradigm. The role of banks is key to this new transition, in which organizations that rely heavily on their supply chain operations are forced to go well beyond their traditional focus on logistics when structuring their networks to take into account the impact of operational transactions on cash flow projections and working capital requirements.

Banks see an opportunity to support their clients in managing the full information–goods–funds loop described in detail earlier.

The financial supply chain encompasses the end-to-end trade processes and information that drive a company's cash, accounts and working capital. The processes that typically need to be tightly linked with the financial chain are, from the buyer's perspective, the procure-to-pay cycle and, from the seller's perspective, the order-to-cash cycle. The goal of the financial supply chain, which I also like to refer to as 'collaborative finance', is to optimize accounts receivable and accounts payable, cash management, working capital and risk.

Supply chain operations must be closely linked with these objectives because of the growing importance of gauging the gaps that appear in these cycles due to the time required to create, transfer and process paper documents. In addition, the cost of errors linked with the manual creation and reconciliation of documentation can no longer be ignored. Increasingly, supply chain managers must also address disputes arising from inaccurate or missing data and the incidence of fragmented point solutions. To do so, they need strong and sustained support from their partners. To shed more light on these issues I spoke to key people at some of the world's major banks whose work has focused on bridging the gap between physical and financial supply chains.

CREATIVE THINKING CREATES NEW ROLES FOR BANKS

One of the leading banks I contacted has formally appointed an individual to head up its supply chain business globally, which shows that the bank takes this sector very seriously. In the past, banks have identified the supply chain solely with procurement, which is the major function they encounter in their daily operations. After all, that function does indeed cover many activities that generate value to a company. For instance, the purchasing of stationery in a bank on average accounts for 20 per cent of the procurement team's efforts. The negotiation of high expenditure contracts for IT systems is another important duty for a bank's purchasing office. A bank also deals with service providers and consultants – some 30 per cent of its efforts is dedicated to managing these high-expense relationships. The last significant element of a purchasing manager's activity in a bank – assuming that this short list covers all of the salient tasks – is purchasing what is usually called 'infrastructure' for outlets and bank branches, also referred to as renovation equipment.

In talking with representatives of major banks I found some had realized, perhaps unconsciously, that banks participate in the planning and control of workflows that match the dynamics of typical physical chains. Let us take the example of the so-called cash supply chain. A bank's cash consists of many elements – cash at its branches, at the cash centre and at the central bank. Cash moves almost constantly across these three locations, and in each it has a totally different cost and return. The cash at the branch can be lent overnight to another bank, but a reserve must be kept locally available for customers. This reserve must not be in excess of the actual customer utilization because it earns nothing for the bank. Excess cash at the branch should be physically moved to the central bank, where it will earn a return, but if there is too little cash it must first go to the cash centre for consolidation. Once the cash is at the central bank it earns a return and can be invested in other instruments – for example, it can be sold to other banks and physically exported there. In the banking business, where physical processes are required to move cash to where the return is greatest, management of the supply chain plays a crucial role.

In fact, one of the most significant and engaging cases involving extremely synchronized cross-border supply chain processes occurred in the collaborative finance domain with the introduction of the euro in 12 EU countries on 1 January 2002. Some 15 different printing works throughout Europe produced the euro banknotes, and physical stocks of banknotes and coins were created for the purpose of the changeover. Almost 80 per cent of banknotes and more than 97 per cent of euro coins – that is 6.4 billion notes and 37.5 billion coins amounting to €133 billion and €12.4 billion – were delivered before E-day. Literally overnight, paper bills of local currency were removed from all ATMs across Europe, and replaced by Euro banknotes. Over the following weeks local-currency banknotes and coins were withdrawn and exchanged. The impact on the supply chain was enormous and prompted some banks to realize that the supply chain is the broader, end-to-end holistic set of processes and practices by which products or services are brought to market, as discussed in Chapter 1.

One leading bank decided to set up a supply chain team because the financial services that cross over with supply chain processes are under close scrutiny from large corporations. There are two main reasons for this. First, many organizations have invested heavily in their physical supply chains and justifiably expect a fair return. Second, close inspection of the procure-to-pay and order-to-cash process flows clearly proves that significant value can be derived from the financial portion of these chains.

The bank's supply chain team offers financial services that support the execution of three key functions. First, it supports transaction management by encouraging the digital exchange of information, which pushes clients towards paperless transactions. This reduces the burden of processing documents manually, especially the letters of credit discussed above. Second, it supports working capital management by improving its clients' cash utilization through facilitating their operations with suppliers, especially those located in the Far East. Pre- and post-shipment working capital finance is the foundation of its portfolio of solutions. Complete visibility of all transactions is, of course, a key element. Finally, the team supports risk management. Like other aspects of supply chain visibility discussed earlier, the mitigation of risk in the daily operations of the supply chain also requires improved visibility, and the same criteria apply when focusing on the level required to properly manage trade risks:

- To whom is the product/service offered?

- What is being offered?

- What payment options are available?

- What shipment will be used?

- What are the reference details of the invoice?

The bank concerned is conscious that buyers are willing to question why they should tie up cash in their balance sheet. The paradigm for the correct management of working capital is to delay payment to suppliers as long as possible – extending DPO. As we saw in Chapter 2, 'choking' suppliers by unilaterally deciding to increase the days of payment is an easy way of extending payment terms. However, this is a short-term remedy because immediately thereafter suppliers will be forced to factor into the cost of materials the consequences of such an arrogant and pushy decision. Throwing the burden of working capital to the other side of the wall is never a wise decision if long-term partnership is the company's strategy.

Nevertheless, working capital certainly benefits from an extension of DPO. Banks entering the supply chain arena take great care to analyse and track a fundamental financial element that has a significant impact on decisions related to working capital management – the cost of capital.

Cost of capital   Cost of capital is defined as a weighted sum of the cost of equity and the after-tax cost of debt. Capital used to fund a business should earn returns for its owners, who have risked their saved money. If an investment is to be considered worthwhile, the estimated return on capital must be greater than the cost of capital. It is relatively easy to calculate the cost of debt, which constitutes the interest paid (interest rate), including the cost of risk. The interest paid by a company will include a risk-free rate plus a risk component, which incorporates the likelihood of default. The cost of equity is broadly considered to be the projected, risk-weighted return required by investors, where the return is largely unknown. This cost, therefore, can be inferred by comparing a particular investment to other investments with similar risk profiles. The cost of equity is sometimes known as the discount rate, as it represents the rate at which projected earnings will be discounted to give a present value. Companies also use the weighted average cost of capital (WACC) plus a risk premium as the figure for the discount rate. WACC will be discussed later in this chapter.

This definition helps us understand that the lower the cost of capital, the lower the financial burden a company will have to sustain for lenders and shareholders. Since a large proportion of the value of cost of capital is related to company and market risk, a large and wealthy company operating in a mature industrial and financial market clearly shoulders less risk and therefore will have a lower cost of capital than a company of similar size that faces operational instability and/or is located in a region of the world where there is greater market insecurity. This mirrors the current situation facing Western companies that initiate trade agreements with suppliers in the Far East or other regions, where labour costs are attractive but are inversely proportional to the financial risk posed by trading with those countries.

The measured gap between the values of the costs of capital of the importing and exporting companies tops an average of 4.7 per cent,[12] which means that the cost of money for a Far East exporter is almost 5 per cent higher than for its corresponding import trade partner. In this light, one major bank has identified a significant role that it can play in ensuring value to both exporter and importer clients, who have contrasting objectives. The exporter (supplier) wants to collect invoiced money as soon as possible to finance its operations – that is, shorten its DSO. The importer (buyer) wants to issue cash as late as possible – that is, increase DPO – to improve the effectiveness of its working capital.

Assuming a likely scenario in which the importer is a Western company and its exporting counterpart is in Asia, the bank can provide value to both sides. For exporters, it pays the invoice immediately at date of issue and allows them to write off the accounts receivable value from their books. For importers, it allows the days of payment contractually agreed with suppliers, thereby benefiting the accounts payable portion of their accounting books.

The bank also benefits, deriving initially from offering better service to its clients and attracting new prospects with this compelling value proposition. By offering such services the bank raises the exit barriers to its clients, thus encouraging greater loyalty and customer retention. Profit also accrues to the

---

12   According to interviews with HSBC executives.

bank from the difference between the full value of the invoice and the discounted value paid to the exporter in relation to the payment days of its contractual agreement with the importer. To illustrate this more clearly, suppose that the importer agrees to pay the exporter's invoice at 45 days and the bank pays the invoice to the exporter immediately at date of issue, discounted for the equivalent value of the 45 days. The bank takes on the risk of anticipating cash to the supplier, having performed a thorough due diligence of the importer's creditworthiness and having established that the risk of non-payment is low and acceptable. This whole process is transparent to the buyer, who benefits from paying at the date of invoice, taking advantage of all the payment days with no pressure from the supplier to anticipate the term. In some cases, the bank might also offer the buyer a delay in payment, thus extending the buyer's DPO to the buyer's whole benefit. Although this process – also known as invoice discounting – is by no means new to banks, its novelty here resides in the use of Internet-based technology platforms that automate the whole process and extend immediate and real-time visibility to the trading partners.

In all this there is a very sensitive financial process of which the bank must be aware. It is crucial that the trade payables should not be converted into bank debt – that is, an obligation on the buyer to repay the financier at maturity of the invoice – since this would have a highly negative effect on the buyer's own debt gearing and potentially on its own credit ratings, rendering the model unattractive from the buyer's point of view. Since the buyer has an obligation to pay the supplier, this must be recorded in its accounts as accounts payable. If the bank finances the supplier, however, the buyer's obligation should shift from a trade payable – accounts payable – to bank debt. Buyers do not like this because, according to the new Sarbanes-Oxley mandate, such a shift of risk to the bank is reflected in a similar risk factor to the company that benefits from the bank's action. This is especially true – and is a major problem – for companies in the US, UK and Australia. Banks, therefore, must find financial solutions that offset such a potentially damaging situation for their clients. The accounting status as a trade payable can be assured through a number of structured financing techniques, such as a robust legal framework and management of the settlement of all a corporation's trade payables at invoice maturity, whether financed or not, possibly through a third-party service provider.

Tracking shipments   The assumption of credit risk from the bank clearly depends on the ability to track each transaction that has implications on the movement of goods for which the bank provides cash finance. The bank must therefore manage the information on the shipment rather than on the goods themselves. Tight collaborative relationships with logistics providers such as DHL, FedEx and UPS can ensure that a bank keeps informed on the current status of shipments.

Such extended insight into supply chain matters offers the bank an opportunity to provide additional value-added services to its top clients by extending its traditional cash and accounting service towards true supply chain collaboration. Take, for instance, what one global bank does for a large UK retail client, which imports goods from the Ukraine. The company does not have a direct subsidiary there to oversee supply chain transactions, so the correlated financial risk would be extremely high and perhaps prohibitive. The retailer's bank, however, does have a subsidiary in the Ukraine, enabling it to take on the role of an intermediary logistics partner. Through a collaborative electronic B2B platform the retailer issues electronic purchase orders to its Ukrainian suppliers. These transactions are then captured by the bank, which manages the orders from a financial and logistical perspective, fulfilling all of its client's obligations.

Other financial institutions prefer instead to service the market by taking a more holistic approach, which involves directly owning, and hence managing, physical transactions. Take, for instance, J.P. Morgan Chase (JPM). Through the acquisition of the global trade management application software provider, Vastera, the bank offers its clients the possibility of managing information and processes in support of the movement of physical goods and financial settlement of the complete global trade process. Through this combination, JPM has been one of the first financial institutions to offer an integrated cash, trade and logistics solution across the physical and financial supply chains. In doing so, JPM has hit upon a market reality – namely, that corporate functions still remain segregated. The common language of working capital can bridge the wide gap between managers of physical flows (supply chain managers) and the managers of financial flows (treasury managers).

With the greater number of links in supply chains and their wider geographical dispersal, clients' concerns about their banks' ability to follow and support them is clearly greater. A bank's capacity to manage trade business lies principally in its ability to help clients move goods across borders without physical and financial disruptions. The value proposition that establishes a bank's competitive differentiation resides in its ability to support clients in the creation and management of 'what-if' cash projection scenarios. We can call this sales and operations planning (S&OP) with cash flow projections.

S&OP with cash flow projections   S&OP is a well-established supply chain management practice and it is well described by the Association for Operations Management as:

> *A process to develop tactical plans that provide management the ability to strategically direct its businesses to achieve competitive advantage on a continuous basis by integrating customer-focused marketing plans for new and existing products with the management of the supply chain. The process brings together all the plans for the business (sales, marketing, and development, manufacturing, sourcing, and financial) into one integrated set of plans. It is performed at least once a month and is reviewed by management at an aggregate (product family) level. The process must reconcile all supply, demand, and new-product plans at both the detail and aggregate levels and tie to the business plan. It is the definitive statement of the company's plans for the near to intermediate term, covering a horizon sufficient to plan for resources and to support the annual business planning process.*[13]

JPM's proposition is to add a projection of cash flows to the projected supply and demand flows of goods. If one considers, say, a plan to launch a new line of cars into a given marketplace it is easy to see some of the key planning elements that must be considered alongside the more traditional analysis of the physical supply chain. These might include how to get paid once the products are sold to the market, how to pay suppliers, how to account for logistics costs and how to take advantage of free-trade zone regulations and offers.

On closer examination it is clear that these are not new business practices. What is new, however, is the means by which these practices must be managed in today's business environment. Sources in most companies' supply chains have changed, and lead times are longer, which increases risk, uncertainty and variability. The direct consequence is that functional silos can no longer work independently. While the tendency for a company's executive management to control and direct the outcomes of the supply chain operations remains unchanged, it is important that people from different parts of an organization take time to understand how they interact and affect each other. The need to identify how the business environment changes dynamically leads us to refer back to working capital. The scenario analysis vital for the deployment of S&OP with cash flow projections opens the way to a new form of working capital analysis – working capital 'in motion'.

---

13 APICS Dictionary, 11th edition, at: http://www.apics.org.

Working capital 'in motion'   The 'people' factor requires that all parties are aligned in their goals and activities, and that they are well aware of all the processes involved. This became abundantly clear from discussions with another representative of a large, global bank whose focus is on best practice.

The bank's stance is informed by extensive analysis of how ERP transactions spanning the creation of purchase orders, good inwards receipts, invoices and payments can facilitate the transition from the physical to the financial supply chain. It has concluded that, to execute the payments representing the financial side of the equation, it is important to understand the underlying physical processes, but it has also found that there is strong resistance from the operators of the physical supply chain, who tend to avoid the responsibility of understanding and measuring the financial implications of their actions, and from their financial supply chain counterparts who are often found to be frightened by the complex, unstructured and often 'maverick' means by which supply chain operations are run.

If net working capital is the compass that orientates the treasury manager's activities, it must be translated into the language of other supply chain parties in order to pull together the requirements and activities of all the different players in the game. The bank, therefore, recommends engineering and deploying structured education programmes to build bridges of common understanding and create a shared language for individuals working in the financial treasury/ accounting departments and the operators of the physical supply chain.

BANKS EMBEDDED IN THE SUPPLY CHAIN

Banks are approaching the physical supply chain from different perspectives. At the Supply Chain Management department of BNP Paribas they describe the bank's more hands-on logistics offer. BNP Paribas is one of the largest international banking networks to have a strong position in Asia, as well as a significant presence in the US. It is another example of a bank that is increasingly prioritizing a focus on supply chain management.

As we have already seen, banks have their own supply chains that are sufficiently complex to require fully dedicated resources and managerial skills. In recent years they have put considerable emphasis on these supply chains, which involve the movement of physical goods and services to their customers, both internal and external. Although a bank's customer offering consists mostly of service, this can often involve the physical delivery of items and therefore the bank must focus on the chain that delivers them to its customers. For example, a customer who opens a bank account expects to receive a customized card to use at ATMs. This clearly involves a physical supply chain, as the card goes through various processes such as printing the base card, sending it to the customization centre, forwarding the relevant secure data file, sending the card to the branch that manages the customer account and so on, until the card is physically shipped and delivered to the customer. These steps necessarily bear the same time pressure as any other supply chain processes. A clear timeframe for delivery is defined by customers' expectations of when they will receive their cards, which they base on the bank's promise to them.

We have previously seen that even the most traditional bank service like the letter of credit involves a significant number of steps, many of which are linked to the management of the physical movements of goods, including the corresponding documents and the letter itself, which engage many parties at various stages. All these processes can be viewed as a supply chain that delivers the letter of credit within the promised timeframe. BNP Paribas goes beyond this simple view to offer real physical services to its customer base that span the management of receivables and inventory, trade transactions between suppliers and buyers, the purchase of receivables from suppliers and the purchase of inventories of goods. In fact, BNP Paribas owns Utexam Logistics Ltd, a multi-client, multi-company, multi-product distribution company based in Ireland.

It is universally known that inventory is a hot potato for both buyers and suppliers. For the reasons relating to the implications for working capital discussed above, suppliers want to convert goods into cash as soon as possible, while, at the same time, buyers want just-in-time deliveries combined with additional flexibility of just-in-case reserves of inventory – off their balance sheet, of course. BNP Paribas has identified an opportunity to place itself between the trading parties. It purchases goods from suppliers and stores them in its Utexam warehouse. It pays the supplier at the date of invoice issue and delivers just-in-time to buyers, billing them at the expiry of the contractual obligation the buyer has originally signed with the supplier. In some circumstances BNP Paribas may decide to allow for a later payment if the buyer's creditworthiness sits within the bank's risk management constraints. The physical handling of goods is not managed directly by Utexam personnel, but by more expert logistic providers such as DHL and FedEx. These agents ensure the correct management, warehousing, handling and transportation services to guarantee the satisfaction of the end client.

While all this looks very nice and almost parallels the business model of more specialized distributors such as Avnet and Ingram Micro, it is not immediately apparent how BNP Paribas generates value. In fact, it does so in two ways. First, the bank leverages the value difference between the cost of purchase and the price at which goods are sold, thanks to the effects of economies of scale and contractual negotiation power. Second, and more relevant to the bank's value, it can arbitrage between the different values of the weighted average cost of capital (WACC).

A bank's WACC is much lower than that which any other company can afford. The difference is somewhere between 6–8 per cent per year for the bank versus a company's 15–25 per cent.[14] The bank takes advantage of what normally happens in a relationship between buyer and supplier. To attain their objective of achieving immediate availability of material with the least impact on their accounts, buyers force suppliers to keep a reserve of stocks always available at no cost to them. The supply chain management practice normally adopted to address this situation is called consignment stock. This is a concept for planning and controlling inventory in which suppliers have access to customers' inventory data and are responsible for maintaining the inventory level those customers require. Vendors resupply through regularly scheduled reviews of on-site inventory. The on-site inventory is counted, damaged or outdated goods are removed, and the inventory is restocked to predefined levels. The inventory value sits on the suppliers' books until buyers physically pick up the goods. As a consequence, suppliers tend to offset the cost of this financial burden, measured by WACC, by increasing the cost of goods by an equivalent amount of WACC. Buyers are therefore charged hidden costs that reflect suppliers' cost of capital. Because suppliers' WACC is almost 20 per cent greater than a bank's, it is immediately evident that an inventory managed by a bank becomes significantly cheaper. There is, therefore, a benefit to buyers purchasing from Utexam.

In reality, the benefits accrue to all parties. Buyers reduce the inventory burden via consignment stock and maintain their DPO value as contractually negotiated with suppliers. The suppliers reduce their days sales outstanding (DSO) and days inventory outstanding (DIO) components of working capital. BNP Paribas creates a competitive edge and a value-added service in its supply chain finance portfolio. If properly managed, this factor increases the competitive advantage obtained from a bank's value proposition. It is, however,

---

14 Author's own research.

important to note that this practice is possible in Europe but not in the US where legislation prohibits banks from owning third-party inventory.

These examples from BNP Paribas and other large banks show, at the very least, that banks are trying to innovate around supply chain issues. Their efforts so far show that bridging the gap between physical and financial supply chains to streamline the flows of goods, funds and information requires them to take a very different perspective on supply chain management and develop a common language with which to discuss its impact on financial measures.

PART II

Metrics and Models

4

How Do Companies Measure the Performance of Their Supply Chains?

The analysis in Chapter 2 of supply chain events that impact on elements of the balance sheet and income statement shows the importance of supply chain management as a strategic corporate asset and demonstrates why the language of finance is becoming more relevant for supply chain professionals. It is the language used by stakeholders, investors and owners to gauge the value generated by a company. The supply chain managers' growing understanding of the financial supply chain has led banks into placing more emphasis on supply chain management, having previously seen it as a peripheral issue. Knowledge and visibility of supply chain transactions are now inherent parts of their strategy to capture more market share and ensure customer retention, which makes bridging the gap between the physical and the financial even more urgent.

There is certainly still a disconnect between the way in which supply chain managers and finance departments measure the performance of their operations. It might be thought that this is due to a lack of appropriate measurement systems, but supply chain managers in fact have a wealth of metrics and key performance indicators at their disposal.

Identifying the Metrics

Supply chain managers need not look far to find the tools to evaluate how well a supply chain is running. A study from the Politecnico di Milano listed over 20 different systems for performance measurement, each of which has its own hierarchies of metrics, submetrics, matrices, frameworks and tables.[1] In some there is a good balance of financial and non-financial indicators. Some systems defined in the study place greater importance on quality; another attributes relevance to questionnaires and to the weighted measurement of the collected subjective results.

The systems outlined in this research may not be the last word on metrics, and precise definitions are likely to vary. There is, in fact, no generally recognized and accepted set of indicators. Nevertheless, there is a vast array of metrics from which supply chain managers can create a system that meets their specific needs. In fact, the research cited above contains an overwhelming number of indicators seeming to suggest unmanageable complexity, but not all of them would be used on a daily basis.

In finance, life is made easier by a more precise set of guidelines in the form of generally accepted accounting principles (GAAP), which clearly outline what performance models to use (balance sheet, income statement and cash flow statement) and which determine the appropriate indicators (accounts receivable, accounts payable, net income and cash from operating activities) in specific sections (assets, liabilities). Supply chain managers are practical people who appreciate simplicity, which is why they tend to measure the same things, although they have different names for the metrics they use. There is little room in their day-by-day duties for tangible/intangible balanced scorecards or indicators that rely too heavily on statistics.

A recent survey,[2] which asked a large number of European companies to list the three most common metrics used in measuring the performance of their supply chains, showed that these vary significantly. Here are some typical examples of the metrics they chose:

- value issued/returned; completeness of order; remanufacture efficiency

- stock; transportation costs; perfect order fulfilment

- supply chain flexibility; supply chain management costs; supply chain assurance and quality

---

1   K. Fahmy Salama, 'Selecting Supply Chain Performance Measurement Systems: A Reference Framework', internal research paper, 2005.
2   Finance Director Europe & Supply, October 2006.

- perfect order fulfilment; costs; delivery accuracy

- stock levels; delivery accuracy; COGS

- sales; planning accuracy; inventory turnaround

- delivery accuracy; delivery quality; partner performance

- DSO; supplier performance index; on-time delivery

- delivery reliability; flexibility; cost

- reliability; costs; inventory level.

There are many factors mentioned above, but if we look a little deeper the responses do at least appear to confirm that efficiency, cost reduction, customer service and delivery performance are the key indicators that supply chain managers use to measure their operations. They also prove, however, that there is no standardized model for naming the metrics. Even when they are referenced with similar terms – as with perfect order fulfilment and delivery accuracy – it cannot be assumed that the results for these seemingly identical parameters are calculated in the same way.

The variance in terms used by supply chain managers for their metrics suggests that a lack of commonly accepted definitions for performance indicators is not an issue that concerns them. This may in fact be true. Standards are not generally high among their priorities. They may well feel that standards are constrictive, serving only to inhibit the free choice, managerial flexibility and intuition on which decision-makers so often rely.

If a company and its supply chain manager are happy to keep an internal focus on the way in which metrics are collected and calculated, they may well find it hard to develop a consistent model that allows them to enhance supply chain management through accurately measuring supply chain performance. It cannot be denied, however, that it may well be a painful process to transform from the status quo, where supply chain analysis provides a historical picture of the supply chain 'as-was', to a more proactive, and possibly even predictive, system which derives from the tracked results of a number of actionable items, each of which contributes to the overall improvement of supply chain performance.

No matter which system a company develops for measuring its supply chain activities, it should not only be simple to use, but also capable of providing salient information on the actions required to move towards a desired objective. It should present this in dashboard format which is far easier to read and interpret. The system should also indicate clearly the correlations between the where, what, how and why – the current status, the desired objectives, the actions required to achieve these objectives and the impact of the measured actions on overall supply chain performance.

The Performance Metric Chart

Having spent many years as a logistics, supply chain and plant manager I have seen many models in action. Of these, I have always preferred, and would recommend, a slight adaptation of the 'BOS chart', which I used during my time as supply chain manager with a Tier 1 automotive supplier..

Figure 4.1 depicts a chart that is built for each of the performance indicators under scrutiny. This in itself already provides a tangible indication that improves the manager's efficiency and effectiveness, insofar as it helps them to avoid the incumbent 'analysis paralysis' that generates from factoring in too many metrics. The need to update the data on a monthly basis for all the four quadrants makes it practically impossible if there are more than four or, at the very most, five metrics to consider. This is true whether the updates are manual or run through the company's ERP. In my case, we ran them all manually using one of the most widely used software applications in supply chain management: the Microsoft Excel spreadsheet.

It is important to remember that supply chain managers must not only read this chart, but also take immediate action in response to the results. The task of collecting and representing the historical data in a useful format is only a fraction of their real work. It is merely the starting-point that triggers all the actions that will be planned, initiated and executed that month or in the near future. Using the time period of one month to refresh and respond to the data provides the right balance between the theoretical need to capture the results on a more frequent basis – perhaps daily – and the practical approach that sees a 'good enough' monthly review of actions that usually take some months or quarters to complete. A continuous refresh of the data would steer the supply chain manager once again towards 'analysis paralysis' in the face of too much data.

KPI: *Delivery Performance*

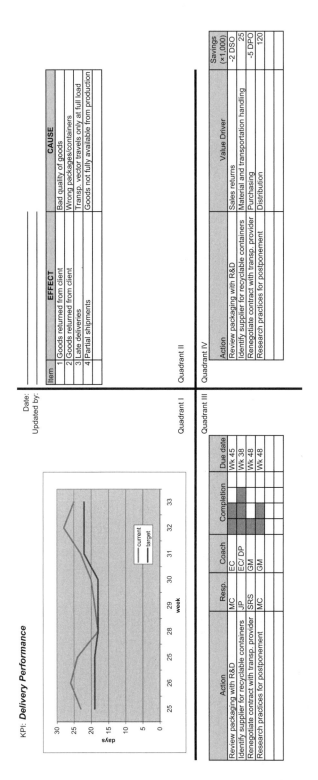

Date:
Updated by:

Item	EFFECT	CAUSE
1	Goods returned from client	Bad quality of goods
2	Goods returned from client	Wrong packages/containers
3	Late deliveries	Transp. vector travels only at full load
4	Partial shipments	Goods not fully available from production

Quadrant I   Quadrant II

Quadrant III   Quadrant IV

Action	Resp.	Coach	Completion	Due date
Review packaging with R&D	MC	EC		Wk 45
Identify supplier for recyclable containers	JP	EC/ DP		Wk 38
Renegotiate contract with transp. provider	SRS	GM		Wk 48
Research practices for postponement	MC	GM		Wk 48

Action	Value Driver	Savings (×1,000)
Review packaging with R&D	Sales returns	-2 DSO
Identify supplier for recyclable containers	Material and transportation handling	25
Renegotiate contract with transp. provider	Purchasing	-5 DPO
Research practices for postponement	Distribution	120

Figure 4.1   Example of a performance metric chart

The bottom line is that even the support of an ERP system, which automatically collects the raw input data, calculates using the formulas and records the resulting performance measurements, would not reduce the effort required from supply chain managers to respond to the data and implement the necessary actions suggested by subsequent analysis. Any decision support tool that proves really effective does so because it gives the decision-maker a much deeper understanding of a situation. It truly realizes its power when it has the ability to provide predictive information.

This kind of predictive capability resides partly in the algorithmic power of the tool, but more importantly in the manager's experience and ability to read between the lines. Automation helps to bring up the numbers immediately, but whether these figures are right or wrong depends not on the speed of the system but on the intelligence of the calculations running behind the scenes. The value of the data then depends on the time and effort dedicated to analysing the numbers the tool produces.

Interpreting the Performance Metric Chart

An explanation of the structure of each of the four quadrants of the chart will help to clarify why I suggest this model as a simple and practical tool for any supply chain manager. I should point out, of course, that all the descriptions I will provide and the entire model could well be applied to functions not directly related to supply chain management. I have, for instance, seen the same structure applied by a human resources manager to track and resolve the causes of workforce absenteeism, and seen a sales manager use this chart format to map and address the effects of customer late payments and returns.

Later, I will provide guidance on how to build, and then use, a performance metric chart.

QUADRANT I: KEY PERFORMANCE INDICATORS (KPIs)

At quadrant I – the top left of the performance metric chart, also known as the KPI quadrant – the dynamic tracking of the key performance indicator is displayed, measured over time. The metric measures the average order fulfilment cycle time from week to week. The constant reference against an expected target value that either comes from a budgeted projection or from a performance objective established within the supply chain function, highlights the need to continuously compare desired versus real situations and to expand the list of possible scenarios that separate the two. It is not uncommon to see companies establish targets derived from industry benchmarks when they have not even completed an internal benchmarking exercise between departments. Automation could certainly help here in plotting the results of a basic set of data that can be complex, especially when the data sources are varied and dispersed across the enterprise. It is true, however, that the data collected usually belong to a specific line of business within the company; so it should be possible to keep the data collection process quick and simple.

Nevertheless, it is important that the sources of data in the performance metric chart are clearly identified and that the data are collected according to a consistent and agreed protocol. For example, if the company wants to track inventory days to measure the performance of its planning and forecasting capabilities, the inventory data should always be collected at a precise instant – perhaps at the end of business of the last day of the month, or any other chosen day, so long as it remains unchanged until the change is planned, discussed and approved.

The choice of how to represent the dynamic of the indicator graphically is not that important, but simplicity is always preferable. Therefore, I suggest a basic linear graph rather than multi-coloured histograms.

QUADRANT II: ROOT CAUSES

Up to this point we cannot say that the information in quadrant I adds more to what is routinely measured and recorded in actual versus desired charts. The real added value of the overall dashboard of the performance metric chart really begins in quadrant II, the 'root cause' quadrant.

Tracking the status of the performance indicator along time is the easy part. It is much harder, but absolutely more valuable, to determine the elements that cause such discrepancies from the target objective. The analysis of the root causes – the fundamental elements that keep the current measurement off target – takes us beyond merely observing the situation towards identifying the most critical areas in which to take action.

At this stage the final action has not yet been decided. Quadrant II is compiled by the user and their team, who use their experience and their research to identify what could have realistically generated the measured results. The originating causes can be either internal (under the control of the supply chain function) or external.

External causes are especially important for two reasons. First, supply chain operators extend their view out of their comfort zone. They must be able to appreciate how external functions impact on their daily activities to the point that a key performance metric is so significantly affected that it deviates from the targeted result. Second , the identification of an external root cause triggers an action item that must be discussed, planned, implemented and resolved in collaboration with the neighbouring department from which the negative effect on the performance metric originated. While it is universally agreed that collaboration is key to success, it is often pursued with external parties, leaving the series of internal islands of power untouched. These islands have usually stratified over time to become sources of internal disconnects and conflicts. Companies usually prefer to use their negotiating power with suppliers or their persuasion on customers rather than trying to find the right balance between corporate functions.

When integrating commercial partnerships, one of the toughest tasks is to manage expectations and ensure that each constituent keeps its promises. But to achieve this, organizations must continually track and measure partner performance and take charge of the process. That is when it becomes clear that control must begin internally. It is impossible to direct external players if the internal business processes are not well managed. Usually, the weakest link resides within the company itself.

This means that a company must take one step back to examine its own internal processes before implementing solutions that support its external collaboration strategy. Only after putting its own house in order will a company be able to evaluate how to execute process collaboration externally in a profitable way. This is why the identification of external root causes requires internal and external partners to speak the same language.

There are many specific techniques that support the analysis and identification of the root causes, but all of the literature sounds one message very clearly: keep it simple. Most studies also recommend that a few relevant items yield better results than a thorough list. The analysis paralysis factor is always lurking in the shadows, and supply chain managers should always be on their guard.

Compiling quadrant II of the performance metrics chart is a major step towards a better understanding of what lies behind the performance of key indicators. It happens as a result of an objective analytical approach, integrated with, and informed by, a healthy dose of instinct which must never be lacking from any managerial decision-making process.

QUADRANT III: THE ACTION PLAN

The value of the time and effort spent on identifying the root causes becomes clear once quadrant III is compiled. Little is gained by preparing a list of negative-effect causes in quadrant II if no attempt is made to reduce or eliminate them. A mere list of grievances, offering no mitigating solutions, would only add to the supply chain manager's frustration.

In quadrant III the team effort must focus on proposing a number of action items that, when implemented, will eliminate – or at least reduce – the causes of underperformance. These actions should be achievable, traceable and closely correlated to the items in quadrant II.

Let us examine each element of quadrant III in turn.

- *Action.* This is the improvement action that the supply chain management team will work on. The list of actions can be identified with the supply chain management project portfolio.

- *Responsible.* Accountability is paramount. Since a number of improvement actions will require collaboration with other company functions, the responsible party takes ownership of the 'political' process that ensures the successful completion of any initiative.

- *Coach.* This is the 'sponsor' of the initiative – that is, the 'facilitator' – who ensures that resources are available. The coach handles the internal politics.

- *Completion.* An action plan requires good planning and completion milestones. This column graphically represents the progress towards the expected due date. Each block corresponds to a 25 per cent completion state, and the darkened blocks show when that level of completion has been achieved. Keeping track of completed actions helps accomplish a positive resolution of the activity in two important ways. First, it gives the supply chain manager an immediate, quantified overview of how far the activity is from its goal. Second, it provides the owner of the activity with an indication of how to organize the remaining time, and it can also be used as an input for a personal capacity plan. This aspect is, of course, also relevant to the supply chain manager, who needs to have a clear view of the team members' commitments and time allocation.

- *Due date*. The time factor once again shows up. Ownership and accountability have their own metric, which is the date by which the action should be completed.

QUADRANT IV: BUSINESS IMPACT

The last piece of the puzzle, the business impact quadrant, builds a bridge across the gap between operations and finance. So far, all the reported information in the performance metric chart relates to operational performance and to areas for improvement suggested by supply chain related KPIs. Measurement, root cause analysis and action lists are all focused on the operational side of the equation and typically reside within the supply chain function. It is important, however, to demonstrate that the effort put into improving the final result of the metric will generate a positive return on overall corporate value. Therefore, the evaluation of the resulting performance must be measured in terms of value creation other than pure cost containment or reduction. This is the point where the notion of linking financial decisions with supply chain performance becomes practical and concrete guidance.

The final quadrant of the performance metric chart is constructed by mapping the results achievable through the items listed in quadrant III with financial indicators found in the balance sheet and income statement. This is the key to the whole exercise of creating the dashboard and the foundation of any approach that aims to measure the supply chain performance by linking financial decisions with it.

Building and Using the Performance Metric Chart

Looking again at Figure 4.1 (p. 99), the first 'how to use' instruction is that a performance metric chart is read from left to right, top to bottom.

Quadrant I represents the 'as-is' picture of the key performance indicator, revealing the distance from the desired target. Quadrant II, at the top right, breaks the indicator down into the root processes and practices that strongly affect the measured results. Internal and external causes represent the levers which the supply chain management team must pull in order to close the gaps.

How to tackle the blocks that keep the gaps open can be deduced by moving from top right to bottom left, where quadrant III compiles the action list and identifies the process owners who will drive the initiative to improve the KPI. Here, collaboration is vital to ensuring success, as is accountability.

Moving to the right brings us to quadrant IV, which condenses the impact of the executed improvement actions into measures of cost savings and value generated.

The best way to appreciate how to practically build and then use the chart is to follow the example below that uses a fictitious set of data. In this case, the performance metric we want to track is delivery performance. Refer to Figure 4.1 (p. 99) as the guide for this example.

QUADRANT I

Quadrant I depicts the value of the indicator over time. Two factors immediately become relevant: the frequency of the collection of data points and the calculation formula to derive the numbers to plot. The frequency is directly linked to the sensitivity with which the company wants to measure its performance. Keeping in mind the caveat that collecting data too frequently only increases confusion and can cause analysis-paralysis, it is sensible to track an indicator at least on a weekly basis.

The key aspects on which to concentrate are what data to collect and how to calculate the final indicator. A performance metric such as delivery performance is prone to disparate interpretations, and internal conflicts can arise often over interpretation. Here is where all the relevant company functions must meet and cooperate constructively to agree on what process tasks are under scrutiny and what transactional events must be captured as baseline data inputs for the calculation. Unless this happens, the inevitable will occur: the sales manager will consider 'delivery' to be the process from the capture of the sales order to the physical offloading of the finished good at the end customer's site; a warehouse manager will assume it to be the sequence of events from the moment the goods are picked from the warehouse to the moment they are loaded on the truck; a supply chain manager will see it as those tasks that proceed from the moment the delivery date and quantities are agreed and finally confirmed with the customer to the moment they arrive in the right quantity and quality at the final destination across one or more intermediate distribution and cross-docking centres; and a quality manager will measure delivery performance in terms of how many process elements have been executed in line with the company's quality assurance policy and compliant to industry-specific and environmental protocols.

The apparently trivial debate over whether the start date for calculating the delivery time coincides with the original delivery date requested by the customer when the sales order was captured or the date that was finally agreed between logistics conceals many hidden dangers.

What would happen to the indicator's performance when, as often happens, a customer calls the supplier's representative to expedite an order that originally was due after the one about to be loaded and shipped from the supplier's dock? A service-oriented attitude and desire to fulfil the customer's request would certainly push the supply chain operative to satisfy the buyer's needs by reprioritizing production and delivery. The goods that were supposed to be delivered that day will be left in a staging area and overtaken by the more urgent last-minute call items. The way in which the overall delivery indicator reflects the true performance of the supply chain operations depends exclusively on what data are captured as inputs for the calculation. If the computation takes into account the original requested date, the effort to better service the client by postponing the delivery of the previous order will not be reflected in the final performance indicator. A poorly established parameter can potentially frustrate the effort to provide a better service.

It is therefore worth closely considering what input data should be collected, particularly if the data are collected automatically by an ERP system. All too often these systems are inflexible, in the short term, in the selection of their database fields. Predefined performance indicators are offered as a value-added feature, which might be valid in the initial phases of the journey towards measuring supply chain performance. Usually the adoption of best-practice performance metrics can help a growing company to learn by doing, but once the practice of keeping track of performance becomes part of everyday business the rigid and framed structure of the database can make it hard to adapt calculations to revised principles. I suggest it is better to refer to the delivery date agreed with the client, because it truly reflects the activity performed by the supplier's supply chain to fulfil customers' expectations.

For each item in this quadrant of the performance metric chart we also need to plot the corresponding target objective. If the budget forecast has been properly executed and the monthly target numbers are not a mere twelfth of the overall figure, the target profile will not result in a straight horizontal line but, rather, a profile that follows the dynamic evolution generated by a company's strategy to increase value and performance. A company that sets a uniform and unchanged target for 12 months inspires neither innovation, nor flexibility, nor change.

QUADRANT II

This quadrant drives the user to analyse the causes of the indicator's poor performance. This root cause analysis should always be performed, even when results are within an accepted tolerance zone. Opportunities for improvement must always be pursued. The comfort zone attitude of 'if it ain't broke don't fix it' is not acceptable in any organization that believes in continuous improvement and wants to be at the cutting edge of innovation. Disruptive events can happen at any time.

There are proven techniques for building trees of correlated and consequential causes, one notable example being the Ishikawa model (see Figure 4.2).

The Ishikawa model – named after its inventor, Kaoru Ishikawa, who first used the technique in the 1960s and also known as the cause-and-effect or fishbone diagram – is essentially a graphic tool used to explore and display opinion about sources of variation in a process.[3] It is used to determine a few key sources that contribute most significantly to the problem being examined, as well as to illustrate the relationships among the wide variety of possible contributors to the effect. The name of the problem to be examined is entered at the right of the diagram at the end of the 'backbone' and, the main possible causes of the problem (the effect) are drawn as bones radiating off. Typically, possible causes are added to the main 'bones', and more specific causes to the radiating 'bones', through brainstorming. When the fishbone is complete, it gives an almost complete picture of all the possible root causes for the designated problem.

---

3   For a simple, effective explanation of the model, see: http://mot.vuse.vanderbilt.edu/mt322/Ishikawa.htm.

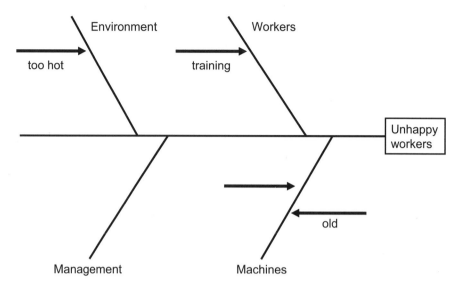

Figure 4.2   Example of an Ishikawa (fishbone) model

Obviously, the tree of causes must also derive from the experience and observations of the manager in cooperation with co-workers. No model, no matter how sophisticated, can replace the need to observe and analyse every detail of any suspicious activity that can hide potentially disruptive inefficiencies. The benefit of using a model like the fishbone resides in its capacity to give the user a structured approach to follow, but this still demands discipline and thorough exploration. Anecdotal observations and events must be filtered through a structured framework in order to provide the relevant statistical evidence for the subsequent improvement actions that will be undertaken.

Our example of how to build a performance metric chart in Figure 4.1 shows that the analysis moves from the undesired effects that are at the basis of poor numbers to their fundamental causes.

One major undesired effect in the example shown in Figure 4.3 is the fact that there are goods returning from customers. This is caused by poor quality of delivered goods, which leads to dissatisfaction and complaints from buyers, who return their purchases and claim refunds. A frequent cause of high customer dissatisfaction is the wrong use of packages or containers. From my experience I can recall many instances where a customer would return goods because of broken containers. Not only do broken containers negate any guarantee that the

Item	EFFECT	CAUSE
1	Goods returned from client	Bad quality of goods
2	Goods returned from client	Wrong packages/containers
3	Late deliveries	Transp. vector travels only at full load
4	Partial shipments	Goods not fully available from production

Quadrant II

Figure 4.3   Performance metric chart: effects and causes section

goods inside have been preserved, but they also highlight a potential risk factor in the plant, where broken parts could cause injuries to material handlers. This is an unacceptable condition that jeopardizes and negatively affects the rate of the delivery performance.

Poor delivery performance is also detected through late deliveries caused by transportation providers who want to travel only at full load in order to offset the direct costs of running the truck. Late deliveries can also occur because the haulier does not have enough space available. This can be the case for non-dedicated transportation services. Local optimization – fully loading the truck – conflicts with the requirements of the vendor, who wants to have enough space available but is indifferent to the transporter's desire for trucks to be fully loaded.

In our example partial shipments signal that deliveries are not achieving the required performance value. This can be for many reasons, but certainly a delayed or postponed shipment caused by lack of material is an all too frequent event.

The delivery problems that I have just described can be mirrored in the case of a service provider. Supply chain management is a disciplined blend of time-based practices and technologies that support users in the design, planning, sourcing, manufacture, delivery, service and return of goods and information relative to products and services delivered in a global market. Services, too, can be returned (not paid for) due to the poor quality of delivery. A performance metric chart can be certainly applied to a service-related metric, such as customer churn, for example.

QUADRANT III

Identifying the root causes of poor performance helps us focus on the key aspects and issues to monitor and resolve. There are no magic silver bullets to make the decisions for us. Managers and their teams must use their experience, along with practices derived from thorough industry research, to select the actions that promise the greatest returns.

It is often the case that the manager decides to source external support in the form of a consultant. An external resource can bring credibility and trustworthiness to the manager's solution plan. Highly innovative activities that promise significant returns are usually seen internally as too ground-breaking and therefore too risky. They are often rejected as pioneering exercises that have no solid business fundamentals.

The beneficial effects that can derive from the supportive input and collaboration of an external resource can only be fully realized by the company if the project team responsible for improving the supply chain is able to control the deployment of the consultant's input. Such control derives primarily from ensuring that the external partner adopts a commonly agreed approach and method. Knowledge-sharing and cross-fertilization must be one of the by-products of the service delivery. A consultant or consulting firm that is too jealous and protective of its models and deployment methods – within acceptable limits of intellectual property protection – brings very little in terms of value creation and knowledge-building. These two factors are quite decisive when selecting the proper partner.

In fact, one of the greatest benefits deriving from joining logistics or supply chain associations is the opportunity to fully exploit the know-how and cooperation of member associates. Their experience of similar situations forms a body of knowledge from which other member companies can take important lessons that will help guide projects, and which provides the confidence that goes with tried, tested and proven practices.

Looking at Figure 4.4, we see how important it is to investigate causes outside the usual departmental comfort zone. Identifying, for instance, that a resolving action requires the renegotiation of contracts with transportation

				Quadrant III	
Action	Resp.	Coach	Completion		Due date
Review packaging with R&D	MC	EC			Wk 45
Identify supplier for recyclable containers	JP	EC/ DP			Wk 38
Renegotiate contract with transp. provider	SRS	GM			Wk 48
Research practices for postponement	MC	GM			Wk 48

Figure 4.4   Performance metric chart: action items section

service providers puts the ball straight into the purchasing manager's court. It thus becomes apparent how sensitive this approach can be, and how much the political support of a senior manager can help with avoiding internal disruptive conflicts that could easily outweigh the benefits of completing the project task. It is therefore good practice to involve all those functional departments with an influence on supply chain operations from the outset. Once again, experience shows that this cooperative effort can be accomplished and turned into a common practice only when the company's senior management puts out a strong message of commitment to the entire organization.

Involving all of an organization's counterparties from the start may seem like common sense and, perhaps, commonplace, but making that a practical, implementable guideline is relatively difficult, principally because each function still speaks its own language and, if they measure the performance of their activities, it tends to be with department-based indicators.

This adds a second layer of complexity to the already challenging role of senior management, as they need to put out directives for stronger collaboration – with clear indicators – that are compelling enough to spur each department into action. Performance results must have common ground. The supply chain manager, measured on the ratio of transportation costs over total company revenue, or sometimes to total costs, must have the same target as the purchasing manager. As the latter is usually measured on the reduction achieved from supplier costs, the collaborative approach will require a joint effort between the two departments and their financial counterpart, all measured under a new indicator: impact on days purchasing outstanding (DPO). As long as the purchasing manager is able to negotiate payment terms with the transportation service provider that positively impact on the working capital element of accounts payable, the supply chain manager can work with the service provider more freely, without the hassle of loading full trucks of goods to reduce the cost/ton ratio.

Agility often requires less than full trucks to be dispatched under pressure from demanding customers who expect no more than the volumes required. Despatching a full truckload would require higher retail discounts to persuade the customer to accept the excess quantity. This would ensure a nice cost/ton figure, but at the expense of two other elements of working capital: accounts receivable, which would increase if the customer rejects the excess quantity, or would at best remain the same, but for a lower income given the effect of discounts on the retail price; and inventory, which would also be negatively affected (that is, increase) if the excess quantity shipped were stored at the third-party logistics (3PL) provider's warehouse, physically distant from the company's premises, but heavily impacting on the company's balance sheet.

QUADRANT IV

In quadrant IV all actions turn into tangible and quantifiable results. It is the end-game of the projected actions for improvement and it reiterates the conceptual definition of supply chain management. Quantifiable returns allow us to establish the validity of the practices we have chosen to close the gaps left open by the identified root causes.

Tangible returns must be expressed in numbers agreed by all parties within the organization. This means that not everything will be turned into a currency value. As shown in Figure 4.5, there are certain activities that bring easily quantifiable returns, especially in relation to production efficiency and operational improvements.

However, Figure 4.5 shows two clear reasons why it is important to express the performance metric chart's results in a form that can be quantified by others, as long as the basic data points are provided by the supply chain manager.

Let us take, as a first example, the line item that reads 'Review packaging with R&D'. The decision to proceed along this action derives from the analysis of the root causes that determined a consistent return of goods from customers. This generates not only a logistical problem in the need to manage the returns, hold them for inspection, repair or discard, then repackage and store them back in, but also an immediate drop back in the accounts receivable office, which will have to put on hold the invoices already sent to the customer and withhold the

Quadrant IV

Action	Value Driver	Savings (×1,000)
Review packaging with R&D	Sales returns	-2 DSO
Identify supplier for recyclable containers	Material and transportation handling	25
Renegotiate contract with transp. provider	Purchasing	-5 DPO
Research practices for postponement	Distribution	120

Figure 4.5   Performance metric chart: estimated savings section

amount as a receivable to collect. This immediately impacts on the balance sheet and also generates additional workload, an invisible and highly unstructured cost that will be reflected at the closure of the income statement as increased sales, general and administrative (SG&A) costs.

The action of reviewing the packaging with the R&D department will bring the expected benefits that mature as an indicator of how many days sales outstanding (DSO) will most likely be saved. As repeatedly asserted throughout this book, supply chain management is a time-based activity. Therefore, everything can and should be expressed using the time factor as the baseline for any measurement.

In this specific case, a supply chain manager already more or less knows how long a returned good will remain at the customer's goods inwards department before being shipped back (at the cost of the supply chain manager's company). He will also know how long it takes the returned good to be transported back for inspection. Experience also helps him estimate the time it will take to actually inspect, repair (or eventually scrap), repackage and store the good back in the warehouse. All this time represents the delay in receiving the customer's payment. This is the DSO figure, the outstanding days of sales.

The figures in quadrant IV of the performance metric chart under the 'Savings' column can be pushed forward to calculate the return in currency value. It is usually enough for the supply chain manager to produce a result that other managers can use as an input to run more precise evaluations in a way that suits their department.

Everything I have discussed above highlights how relevant it is for a supply chain manager to capture the important data points that colleagues in other departments can evaluate. This will clearly show that the supply chain manager can speak the right language.

We could also examine the value of savings from the action 'Renegotiate contract with the transportation provider'. As mentioned earlier, this decision could certainly generate a strong internal conflict if it is not properly managed. The expected savings figure provides clear evidence that the organization's management has succeeded in getting everyone reading from the same page, even though they previously had different targets.

There is no need for a currency amount to quantify the estimated result. The joint effort between the supply chain manager and the purchasing manager in renegotiating transportation tariffs with the service provider leads to a reduction of payment days to the supplier, measured by the negative DPO figure shown in Figure 4.5. It is negative because a reduction of payment days corresponds to a shorter time in which the supplier gets paid. In other words, the company has to cash out the supplier earlier than before – exactly five days before in our example.

Yet, this apparently counterproductive result on the company's working capital is offset by the possibility that the supply chain manager could ship the goods more flexibly in the sole quantities required by the client. And we have seen previously how much it would cost the company to ship full truckloads for the only benefit of reducing the cost/ton ratio.

Of course, a diligent cost–benefit analysis must be run. In some cases, it may be advisable to get support from people working in the accounts receivable and payable offices in order to identify the proper input data for calculation.

So far, the connections between operational excellence and financial results in the model are almost only related to cost containment and reduction. This is fine, as cost reduction does indeed positively affect the bottom line of the profit and loss statement. However, shareholders, investors, board members, CEOs and financial managers measure the success of programmes and projects in the light of the balance sheet and working capital.

Measuring the Impact of Operations on Finance

It seems that the key aspect of a performance metric chart is the shift from operational measurements and improvements to the more value-based evaluation in quadrant IV. The underlying assumption that makes this shift possible is the ability to map operational practices with financial indicators.

This exercise is certainly possible once it becomes clear that what is important is not a statistically proven set of quantitative factors that establishes the correlation between operations and finance, but the confidence that supply chain and finance executives have that the mappings are generally accepted, validated and reviewed by a community of peers. Once available, this is what can be practically called a 'cost chart' for supply chain managers, and it will then be up to the individual company to populate the correlation table with numbers and factors that derive from a shared and cooperative effort between different internal departments.

Large enterprises typically operate dozens of different business units and extensive production or service operations, each with hundreds of managers and thousands of employees. These corporate divisions, business units, departments, executives, managers and employees have clearly defined roles within the organization, and all business units and employees typically have concrete qualitative and quantitative objectives based on the corporate strategic and operational plans. Quantitative operational and financial objectives are difficult to manage and difficult to predict. Thousands of unique parameters and financial variables affect a company's financial performance and its consolidated financial statement.

Forward-thinking CEOs must be prepared for dynamic change. Management must therefore have at its disposal the right decision support systems to allow managers at all levels to continuously monitor performance and determine compliance, or deviation, from predefined corporate operational and financial objectives. The ability to control dynamic and unpredictable conditions and turn them into competitive advantage only becomes possible when the CEO can take command of decisions that bring rapid results.

Decision support system tools enable the CEO to:

- continuously monitor performance of all corporate units

- discover, in real-time, emerging problems

- pinpoint the source of the problem

- quantitatively assess the impact of the problem if allowed to continue unabated

- formulate corrective action

- quantitatively assess the impact of such action.

Cost savings are not the major process benefits that stimulate the interest of C-level executives, especially CEOs and CFOs. Rather, they want a complete, unified perspective on all the financial and business activities, even those that take place beyond the borders of the company. They want to be able to analyse existing interactions between relevant variables, how they might affect other elements of their business, and how this correlation may affect the consolidated income statement and balance sheet.

Some companies have become quite sophisticated in this process.

CASE STUDY: STRAUSS

Strauss[4] is an emerging international leader in the branded food and beverage industry. With a homebase in Israel, Strauss employs approximately 8800 people, manufactures hundreds of products and operates in five continents.

The company has implemented a 'Control-and-Command Business Platform' based on a software solution that enables executives and managers at all levels to leverage the power of on-time analysis; to more efficiently execute the corporate, divisional and departmental business strategies; to identify operational and financial problems as they occur; and to better predict future operational and financial performance on the basis of real-time performance indicators.

One of the key constituents of this Control-and-Command Business Platform software is the 'Formula Builder'. The business manager's success is measured on the profit margin generated by the operations for which that manager is responsible. The ability to model the business environment conditions and generate the right on-time information would support this task. This is possible through the Formula Builder, which speaks the manager's business language while taking care of the 'backstage' connections and interrelations between data sources and business logic. As an example, a business manager may decide, based on his experience, that a 92 per cent availability of a specific retail product line ensures the minimum level of excess returns from the market, while ensuring the desired profit margin. In

---

4   http://www.strauss-elite.com.

cooperation with the company financial analysts and controllers who 'own' the knowledge of the correlations between the functions, the manager uses the Formula Builder to create this scenario. The system creates a formula that manages the intricacies of the factors across all the data sources that interconnect with the formula elements.

The generic representation of this formula is given below:

$$F(x) = \frac{\sum \text{Expenses}}{\sum \text{Revenues}}$$

The system measures the impact of the operational expenses on the generated revenues. There are multiple sources of expenses and revenues across the entire organization. It is the ability of the business analyst to capture these interdependencies and build the 'tree' of the departmental formulae (see Figure 4.6), which will feed the mathematical algorithms of the Control-and-Command Business Platform. The software platform ensures consistency of results by using one single basic formula to calculate the final

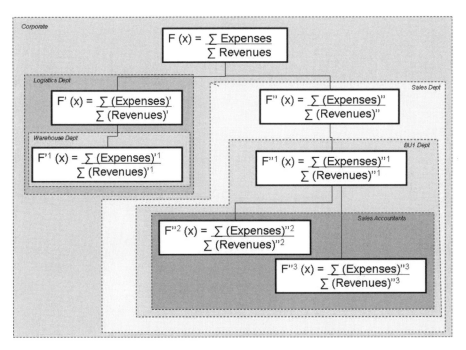

Figure 4.6   A tree of departmental formulae

figures. The different business models interconnected by the formula tree are used and seen by different people within the same organization, depending on their roles and responsibilities. This cascade of correlated formulas can be applied to supply chain management related processes to build the network of key performance metrics.

5

The SCOR™ Model

Detailed research into performance metrics that tie operational excellence to working capital and balance sheet figures has resulted in a model that is widely recognized as the industry *de facto* standard for supply chain management process modelling, performance management and best practices – namely the Supply Chain Operations Reference (SCOR™) model developed and managed by the Supply Chain Council (SCC).

The SCC is a non-profit group founded in 1996 by two US-based advanced firms, the manufacturing consulting company Pittiglio Rabin Todd & McGrath (PRTM) and industry research company AMR Research, and initially it included around 70 companies. Its purpose was to devise improved business process models for the supply chain that could be implemented across a variety of industries, and which would be supported by a complete set of agreed-upon metrics and best practices.

The model is based on three major pillars: process modelling, performance metrics and best practices.

Process Modelling

On the highest level (Figure 5.1), the SCOR™ model is extremely simple, comprising only five Level 1 master 'sub-processes': (1) Plan, (2) Source, (3) Make, (4) Deliver and (5) Return. The model has become slightly more complex over time, but it still captures the essence of the supply chain process. It has proven simple enough, yet sufficiently robust, to be the basis for an entire business process methodology and its associated measurement activity.

In the Level 1 SCOR™ model the components >Source>, >Make>, >Deliver> represent the basic value chain, while >Plan> and >Return> represent control and feedback for the model.

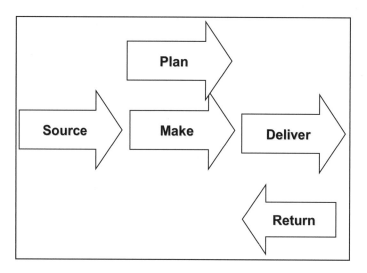

Figure 5.1   The SCOR™ Level 1 model

Within the SCOR™ model there are three primary hierarchical levels (see Figure 5.2).

Level 1 (Model) defines scope, context, geographies, segments and products. This is the highest level of the SCOR™ model and describes the basic functions of supply chain: Source (purchasing), Make (manufacturing, fabrication), Deliver (warehousing, shipping and transportation), Return.

Level 2 (Strategies) identifies strategies within geographies, segments and products. Here, the model really describes the primary manufacturing strategy – do you make (that is, assemble) to order as does Dell Computer or make to inventory? Or do you engineer to order like a job shop? The lower levels of the SCOR™ model will be quite different, depending on a company's choice of manufacturing strategy.

Level 3 (Process-Activities/Metrics/Best Practices) identifies key business activities within any given configuration. This describes the classic business processes (activities) within each of the basic strategies. It is at this level that one can apply performance metrics and best practices.

At Level 1 in particular, the model appears to be simple, but it is at Level 2 that SCOR™ becomes really useful. Level 2 allows the model to be entirely different between an organization that uses classic MRP (Materials Requirements Planning – a software-based production planning and inventory

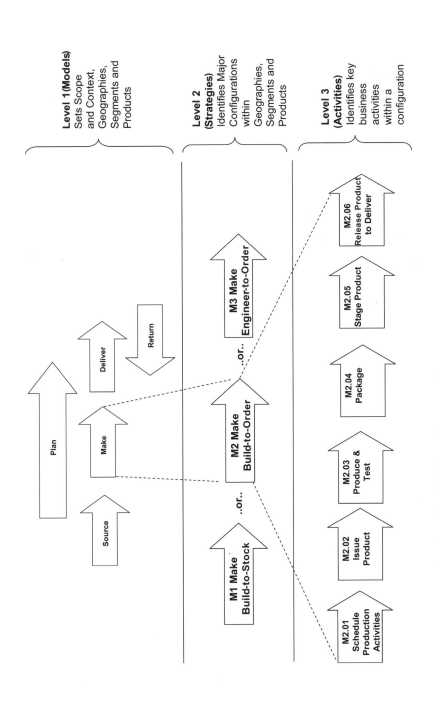

Figure 5.2   **The three levels of the SCOR™ framework**
Source: Joe Francis, PCOR.

control system used to manage manufacturing processes) to forecast required inventory (build-to-stock) and one that makes to order (build-to-order) or makes highly specialized products (engineer-to-order). This feature of SCOR™ allows for three major versions of the same overall model to exist side by side. In fact, it is possible to have all three major strategies working in different divisions of the same organization.

Furthermore, in the overall SCOR™ framework, there are two other levels below Level 3 which deal with specific workflow implementation of the business processes. Activities identified in the SCOR™ model at Level 3 are then implemented through the workflow and other attendant application structures that might also be involved.

What I want to focus on are the two other pillars of the model: the operational performance metrics and the best practices. These are closely correlated in the model, and I will use them as the framework for building a model that will link operational metrics with balance sheet and working capital figures. Also, the fact that the operational metrics and best practices derive from the contribution of SCC members who give up part of their time to join working groups in order to share knowledge and experiences that are then reviewed by their peers makes the framework much more credible and independent from any bias or improper influence.

The SCOR™ Model Performance Metrics

When the first SCC members gathered together and began to discuss how to represent the performance of a supply chain they faced the challenge of deciding what attributes would best describe it. Just as a physical object can be represented through attributes such as length, width, height, weight and colour, the SCC members selected five attributes, which could characterize the performance of a supply chain. These are known as performance attributes and are shown in Figure 5.3.

As expected in a standard model, each attribute is clearly defined in order to avoid any confusion or misinterpretation. However, it immediately emerges that these attributes measure the operational performance of the supply chain under potentially conflicting scenarios.

Performance Attribute	Performance Attribute Definition	Level 1 Metric
Supply chain reliability	The performance of the supply chain in delivering: the correct product, to the correct place, at the correct time, in the correct condition and packaging, in the correct quantity, with the correct documentation, to the correct customer.	Perfect order fulfillment
Supply chain responsiveness	The speed at which a supply chain provides products to the customer.	Order fulfillment cycle time
Supply chain flexibility	The agility of a supply chain in responding to marketplace changes to gain or maintain competitive advantage.	Upside supply chain flexibility
		Upside supply chain adaptability
		Downside supply chain adaptability
Supply chain costs	The costs associated with operating the supply chain.	Supply chain management cost
		Cost of goods sold
Supply chain asset management	The effectiveness of an organization in managing assets to support demand satisfaction. This includes the management of all assets: fixed and working capital.	Cash-to-cash cycle time
		Return on supply chain fixed assets
		Return on working capital

Figure 5.3   Performance attributes of the SCOR™ model

If we take, for example, a sales manager and a financial manager and ask them to indicate which attributes they would select to show how they would like their company's supply chain to perform, the former would certainly point to responsiveness and flexibility in order to fulfil customers' expectations. Conversely, the financial manager would point to cost and asset management aspects to satisfy his 'clients' – investors and shareholders.

Another immediate consideration that requires further evaluation is the fact that no company has just a single supply chain. Beyond the generally accepted principle that we should refer more to a supply network rather than a chain, a more relevant characterization must be formed to fully exploit the power of the SCOR™ performance attributes.

A product that is about to be launched in the market requires full-steam marketing and promotion. Product cycles are shortening and markets are increasingly dynamic, so time-to-market and time-to-volume are key drivers of success. The vendor must confirm its ability to keep its promise to ensure reliable deliveries, responsiveness to immediate fluctuations in demand, and flexibility to adapt to changing customer preferences.

A mature product is one that has already attained its market share and position. All efforts to make it desirable have been deployed, and it sits at the inflection point of the maturity curve (Figure 5.4) before declining into obsolescence. At this point there is no real sense in putting additional effort and resources into shaping a supply chain that ensures flexibility of deliveries and responsiveness to customer demand. The market has a precise opinion of the vendor's reliability in terms of this particular product and little more can be done to change the situation. This means that, after the initial steps of introduction and growth, it makes sense to concentrate on efficiency and exploiting economies of scale to recover the inevitable losses experienced during the initial launch of the product in the market. The same considerations can apply to the life cycle of a single product.

There are as many supply chains to potentially serve the successful delivery of the product to the market as there are different steps of its maturity curve. Reliability is key during the testing and prototyping phase. Supplier sourcing and evaluation, process engineering, design-to-cost criteria, production and logistics flow, material handling and quality assurance, make or buy decisions, channel distribution partners, demand patterns and capacity plans must all be well shaped.

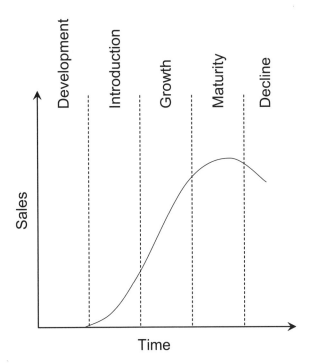

Figure 5.4   The product maturity curve
Source: http://www.netmba.com/marketing/product/lifecycle.

Once the product has been launched in the open market, responsiveness and flexibility become the necessary attributes of a supply chain if it is to ensure rapid time-to-market, availability of items, readiness to respond to customer expectations, and sufficient agility to respond to market feedback from channel and distribution partners, user groups or consumer committees.

When the initial launch has reached its peak, the supply chain must be reshaped in order to capitalize on those factors that contribute efficiency in the production cycles, distribution flows, commercial promotions and the management of the equipment and assets that contribute to the product's success. At this stage of its life cycle the product has lost its initial propulsive energy, and the gradient of the maturity curve rises less steeply. The phases of growth and maturity of Figure 5.4 are key to the product's longevity in the marketplace. It is now payback time for the company that has invested energy and resources in the initial ramp-up phase.

Commercial deals with suppliers and channel partners must now mature to deliver the expected benefits. Production models and material-handling policies must reach full operational efficiency and contribute to lowering the fixed portion of the invested capital. Cost control and containment, together with more disciplined asset management, are the attributes now required to measure supply chain performance.

Once the derivative of the life-cycle curve turns negative – the decline stage of Figure 5.4 – the main indicators to track are the residual life value of the assets and their corresponding levels of amortization, as these contribute to any assessment of the product's eventual success.

It must never be forgotten that the net operating profit of a sales campaign is only one of the evaluation factors that determine the financial success of any initiative. The balance sheet, with its section on liabilities, and the working capital structure, with its references to receivables, payables and inventory, holds the majority of indicators that have the final say on the overall success of the product release.

One essential consideration surfaces from this simple analysis. It becomes obvious that the decision on how a supply chain should perform is not one that lies solely with the supply chain manager. It requires a company strategic evaluation, a commitment and a debate that leads to identifying the key attributes that create the foundation of the supply chain's operational performance.

This long digression on the SCOR™ model and its performance attributes is very important. Our objective is to find a way to link financial decisions with supply chain performance in the most unbiased and independent manner possible. There is a risk of making didactical propositions that, while neatly put forward, are scarcely applicable. Also, the lack of strong supporting literature and consolidated ways of thinking on the subject has contrasting effects. On the one hand, it opens up the opportunity to explore previously untapped areas of discussion. On the other hand, it is still vulnerable to criticism on account of the lack of case studies that might confirm the validity of its findings. In this latter respect building a conceptual framework on the foundations of an independent and *de facto* industry standard model – the SCOR™ model – gives the necessary confidence. If I can find the elements of my proposition in the model – a model that is developed, used and validated by numerous international organizations – then the danger of falling in the trap of the 'nice-to-haves' will be dramatically reduced, if not completely eliminated. To achieve this, of course, all the relevant elements of the model must be accepted and used. And where the model – which, like all things, has limitations – ceases to provide material and content, the direction indicated by the same philosophy and premises that were – and are still – at its foundation can be followed. In other words, advantage can be taken of the continuous contribution and collaboration of supply chain practitioners who offer their time, experience, energy and passion to develop concepts from inception and help them evolve through peer review until they turn into generally accepted guidelines for others to follow.

The purpose of the research that supports this book is to look at ways of building a bridge between the ways in which performance is measured in the operational and the financial side of the organization. This is all well sustained by the SCOR™ model. In fact, the model contributes not only by exposing the attributes of supply chain performance, but also by presenting how each of the attributes can be practically measured. A company's decision to shape its supply chain, whether for the whole organization or for a product in a specific stage of its life cycle, around one of the five attributes of the SCOR™ model would be of little use if management could not effectively know if and when their targets were achieved.

Making a strategic decision that the supply chain organization must be structured to ensure reliability is of little help unless all interested parties understand how to measure their accomplishment of such a challenging objective. Put simply, to be practically effective each performance attribute must be measurable. Furthermore, the measurement must be calculated with a formula (or algorithm) that is absolutely free from any influence or bias. If, for instance, the metric for reliability were chosen as the number of orders delivered on time, in quantity and in quality over the total number of valid orders, then this could easily give rise to misinterpretations and perhaps disputes since, in its simple declaration, the metric is not clear enough on the date of delivery. Should this be the date of shipment from the supplier's shipping bay, or should it be the date of reception at the buyer's dock? And what happens if the buyer has changed the original date after rescheduling? Should the original delivery date be used or should it change? The supplier would certainly want it to reflect the new situation after the buyer's request. But would the buyer agree? Is a new negotiation required each time a delivery date is rescheduled? And what should happen if the supplier requests a postponement of the delivery date and the buyer accepts the delay?

Each party involved would give opposing answers. The buyer and supplier would be unlikely to pick the same dates if they were to choose solely on the basis of gaining maximum advantage. The tug-of-war based on what dates to consider in the evaluation could go on forever, unless both sides can either reach a mutual consensus or agree to join a wider group of peers with whom to establish a common platform for discussion. Such a group must submit to its participants a set of measurements that equally balance opposite interests in the name of a collaborative relationship. These measurements must be based on commonly accepted metrics, which become the standard reference point for the community.

It soon becomes apparent that a standard metric must cover as many alternative scenarios as possible. That's where the incomparable value of SCC's experience emerges, as the common consensus condensed into the SCOR™ model determines rules on how to engage, manage and measure typical situations that occur every day in modern organizations. All of this peer-reviewed common sense is reflected in the last column of Figure 5.3, the Level 1 metric column.

The SCC proposes the SCOR™ model as a practical manual based on the practices and methods of its members. The need for unbiased measures is met by a set of metrics that follow the typical hierarchical structure of the model. The metrics indicated as Level 1 in Figure 5.3 are the parents (the highest level of aggregation) of a breakdown structure on lower-level metrics. These are typically referred to as Level 2 metrics to signify their dependency on the higher-level parent.

A Description of the SCOR™ (Release 8.0) Level 1 and Level 2 Metrics

The Level 1 and Level 2 metrics of the SCOR™ model need to be described in detail because the bridge I want to build between operational indicators and more financially-oriented ones requires an understanding and analysis of what these attributes measure.

So, what financial indicators will be mapped with these supply chain performance attributes? As already discussed it is important to speak the language of finance, which is aligned to working capital and economic profit. Both these indicators constitute elements of the balance sheet and income statement reports.

Chapter 2 demonstrated the importance of supply chain management as a strategic corporate asset by analysing the impact supply chain operations have on the balance sheet and income statement. In order to build the bridge we must, therefore, understand which supply chain management operations we want to measure. The answer lies in the SCOR™ metrics.

I will use the original definitions from the SCOR™ model to ensure consistency. The metrics listed below do not constitute the entire portfolio of Level 1 and Level 2 SCOR™ metrics, as I have selected the ones that present a clear measurement of supply chain operations and their impact on financial results.

- *Level 1 metric (parent) – Perfect Order Fulfilment*: the percentage of orders meeting delivery performance with complete and accurate documentation and no delivery damage. Components include all items and quantities on-time using the customer's definition of on-time, and documentation such as packing slips, bills of lading, invoices.

  - *Level 2 metric (child) – Percentage of Orders Delivered in Full*: the percentage of orders in which all the items are received by customer in the quantities committed. This is calculated by the number of orders that are received by the customer in the quantities committed divided by the total number of orders.

  - *Level 2 metric (child) – Delivery Performance to Customer Commit Date*: the percentage of orders that are fulfilled on the customer's original commit date.

  - *Level 2 metric (child) – Documentation Accuracy*: the percentage of orders with on-time and accurate documentation to support them.

  - *Level 2 metric (child) – Perfect Condition*: the percentage of orders delivered undamaged and meeting specification, have the correct configuration, are faultlessly installed and accepted by the customer.

- *Level 1 metric (parent) – Order Fulfilment Cycle Time*: the average actual cycle time consistently achieved to fulfil customer orders.

  - *Level 2 metric (child) – Source Cycle Time*: the average time for Source processes.

- *Level 2 metric (child) – Make Cycle Time*: the average time for Make processes.

- *Level 2 metric (child) – Make Deliver Time*: the average time for Deliver processes.

• *Level 1 metric (parent) – Upside Supply Chain Flexibility*: the number of days required to achieve an unplanned, sustainable 20 per cent increase in quantities delivered.

- *Level 2 metric (child) – Upside Source Flexibility*: the number of days required to achieve an unplanned, sustainable 20 per cent increase in quantity of raw materials.

- *Level 2 metric (child) – Upside Make Flexibility*: the number of days required to achieve an unplanned, sustainable 20 per cent increase in production, assuming no raw material constraints.

- *Level 2 metric (child) – Upside Deliver Flexibility*: the number of days required to achieve an unplanned, sustainable 20 per cent increase in quantity delivered, assuming no other constraints.

- *Level 2 metric (child) – Upside Source Return Flexibility*: the number of days required to achieve an unplanned, sustainable 20 per cent increase in the return of raw materials to suppliers.

- *Level 2 metric (child) – Upside Deliver Return Flexibility*: the number of days required to achieve an unplanned, sustainable 20 per cent increase in the return of finished goods from customers.

• *Level 1 metric (parent) – Upside Supply Chain Adaptability*: the maximum sustainable percentage increase in quantity delivered that can be achieved in 30 days.

- *Level 2 metric (child) – Upside Source Adaptability*: the maximum sustainable percentage increase in raw material quantities that can be acquired/received in 30 days.

- *Level 2 metric (child) – Upside Make Adaptability*: the maximum sustainable percentage increase in production that can be achieved in 30 days, assuming no raw material constraints.

- *Level 2 metric (child) – Upside Deliver Adaptability*: the maximum sustainable percentage increase in quantities delivered that can be achieved in 30 days, assuming no constraints on finished good availability.

- *Level 2 metric (child) – Upside Source Return Adaptability*: the maximum sustainable percentage increase in returns of raw materials to suppliers that can be achieved in 30 days, assuming no constraints on finished goods availability.

- *Level 2 metric (child) – Upside Deliver Return Adaptability*: the maximum sustainable percentage increase in returns of finished goods from customers that can be achieved in 30 days.

• *Level 1 metric (parent) – Downside Supply Chain Adaptability*: the reduction in quantities ordered sustainable at 30 days prior to delivery with no inventory or cost penalties.

- *Level 2 metric (child) – Downside Source Adaptability*: the raw material quantity reduction sustainable at 30 days prior to delivery with no inventory or cost penalties.

- *Level 2 metric (child) – Downside Make Adaptability*: the production reduction sustainable at 30 days prior to delivery with no inventory or cost penalties.

- *Level 2 metric (child) – Downside Deliver Adaptability*: the reduction in delivered quantities sustainable at 30 days prior to delivery with no inventory or cost penalties.

• *Level 1 metric (parent) – Total Supply Chain Management Costs*: the sum of the costs associated with the SCOR™ Level 2 processes of Plan, Source, Deliver and Return.

- *Level 2 metrics (child) – Cost to Plan, Cost to Source, Cost to Make, Cost to Deliver, Cost to Return*: these measure the global sum of the costs related with their associated processes.

- *Level 1 metric (parent) – Return on Supply Chain Fixed Assets*: the return an organization receives on its invested capital in supply chain fixed assets, which includes the fixed assets used in Plan, Source, Make, Deliver and Return.

  - *Level 2 metric (child) – Supply Chain Fixed Assets*: the return an organization receives on its invested capital in supply chain fixed assets, including the fixed assets used in Plan, Source, Make, Deliver and Return.

- *Level 1 metric (parent) – Return on Working Capital*: assesses the size of investment relative to a company's working capital position against the revenue generated from a supply chain. Components include accounts receivable, accounts payable, inventory, supply chain revenue, cost of goods sold and supply chain management costs.

  - *Level 2 metric (child) – Asset Turns*: total gross product revenue/ total net assets.

  - *Level 2 metric (child) – Order Fulfilment Costs*: includes costs for processing the order, allocating inventory, ordering from the internal or external supplier, scheduling the shipment, reporting order status and initiating shipment.

Best Practices from the SCOR™ Model

Having a list of metrics and ways to calculate with them takes us only halfway to our goal. The real value of a measurement system is that it allows us to gauge the distance between the actual results and the expected ones, the latter having been established by the company board. They are not only an issue for the supply chain manager, but also stem from a broader set of strategic decisions.

As powerful as a metric system can be in terms of the sophistication of its calculations or its ability to factor in intangible elements, it is of little value in business decision-making if it is does not also generate guidelines on how to close the gaps once they are measured.

While a metric system helps to put under scrutiny poor performances or areas that need strong intervention for an improvement, the system alone does not suggest *how* to make the changes.

Guidance on *how* to achieve the right changes comes in the form of best practices.

A *practice* refers to a way in which something is done. Most commonly, practice is a learning method, the act of repeatedly rehearsing a behaviour for the purpose of improving or mastering it. This definition suggests that a best practice helps a company reap the benefits of other companies' experiences. In other words, the company does not have to reinvent the wheel.

Examples of practices abound in research literature. They become best practices when they are widely acknowledged and used in an industry, and when the results are proven to be significantly affecting value and efficiency. A best practice is defined by the SCC in the *SCOR™ Model Book* as a 'current, structured, proven and repeatable method for making a positive impact on desired operational results'.

'Current' means that it must not be emerging, yet must not be antiquated. 'Structured' describes a practice that has a clearly stated goal, scope, process and procedure. A practice is 'proven' when its success has been demonstrated in a working environment. 'Repeatable' means that the practice has been proven in multiple environments. The term 'method' is used in its broadest sense to indicate business process, practice, organizational strategy, enabling technology, business relationship, business model and information or knowledge management. A positive impact on desired operational results occurs when a practice shows operational improvement in its progress towards its stated goal and this could be linked with more than one key metric. The impact should show either as gain – an increase in speed, revenues or quality – or as a reduction in factors such as resource utilizations, costs, loss and returns.

EXAMPLES OF BEST PRACTICE

One good example of a best practice in supply chain management is carrier agreements. These are agreements between a company and its domestic and global carriers of both inbound raw materials and outbound finished goods. They specify service levels and payment terms along with other conditions, and they can be established as part of a larger initiative to decrease raw material and finished goods inventory, while improving customer service.

Cross-docking is another best practice used in many distribution centres to increase inventory velocity while maintaining shipping efficiency. Wikipedia defines it as a practice of unloading materials from an incoming semi-trailer truck or rail car and loading these materials in outbound trailers or rail cars, with little or no storage in between. This may be done to change type of conveyance, or to sort material intended for different destinations, or to combine material from different origins. In a traditional distribution centre the receiving process is disjointed from the shipping process and storage acts as an intermediary between the two. Cross-docking actively links the receiving and shipping processes.

Another example is postponement or delayed differentiation. This is a supply chain concept whereby a product is kept as long as possible in a generic 'neutral' state. Differentiation of the generic product into a specific end-product is shifted closer to the consumer by postponing identity changes, such as assembly or packaging, to the last possible point in the supply chain.

These examples of best practices should make it clear why they are closely associated with performance metrics. As anticipated, and now more strongly proven, the best practices of supply chain management provide practical guidance and direction on how to reduce the difference between the 'as-is' measured and the 'to-be' targeted performance.

The rich list of metrics I have described is the gateway to measuring the operational performance of the supply chain and bridging it to the company's financial indicators. However, a system of metrics, while necessary, is not sufficient in itself to effectively sustain business decisions unless it is connected to practices that offer a route out of inefficiency. The same applies to financial performance if gauged only by metrics. It is important to identify actions that indicate *how* to close eventual financial gaps.

Before proceeding, I must make it clear that we have made an important assumption. The actions that impact on financial performance to which I refer are operational in nature, but there are other actions of a purely financial nature that can significantly affect a company's financial results. These include investments in financial instruments, funding decisions from capital expenditures and allocation of treasury resources. They lie, however, outside of the scope of this book.

Linking Operational Decisions with Financial Performance

Metrics and practices must go hand-in-hand. That much is clear. Furthermore, both must be widely adopted and recognized in the market. What, then, is the logical sequence that leads from operational decisions to financial performance?

This can be better explained if we walk backwards along the chain:

- Financial performance is consequent to the results collected from financial metrics.

- Financial metrics are mapped to operational metrics.

- Operational metrics assess the operational status of the company and are linked to operational decisions which are implemented through practices that are proven to reduce the gap between a poor 'as-is' and a more remunerative 'to-be' situation. A remunerative situation is what shareholders, investors, analysts and owners seek to obtain from the company, so they measure performance from a purely financial perspective.

- A positive result confirms the good quality of the operational decisions taken to accomplish it.

- A negative result highlights the immediate need to take action.

The company must be able to show the course of action it intends to adopt to close the gaps. These actions must prove to be effective and, at the same time, must give stakeholders confidence that they are current, structured, proven and repeatable. There is no time to run experiments. A solid action plan is required to get the metric back on track. This is additional evidence that financial performance and operational decisions are indeed closely linked.

There is one node in the flow that must be proven in order to ensure the existence of the causal relationships between financial performance and operational decisions – the mapping of financial metrics to operational metrics. I have already selected the operational metrics that will be used to establish this mapping exercise: the SCOR™ Level 1 and Level 2 metrics previously described.

Their financial counterparts are the following elements from the balance sheet and income statement:

From the income statement

- *Sales.* This is the top-line figure *par excellence* of the income statement. It is clearly directly related to the way in which supply chain operations are performed.

- *Sales returns and allowances.* This figure deducts the overall revenue value of sales. The correlation with supply chain operations, especially distribution and logistics, is obvious.

- *Cost of goods sold.*

- *Selling, general and administrative (SG&A) expenses.* Indirect expenses are those most appropriate to gauging whether or not supply chain operations are run efficiently. All 'hidden' costs pile up under this figure to generate unwelcome surprises in the year-end financial report.

From the balance sheet

- *Inventories.* This is another financial item *par excellence* that clearly puts the supply chain under the microscope.

- *Accounts receivable.* This represents the amount of money owed from the customers. It is a clear sign of the supply chain management team's ability to fulfil demand expectations and its value could be excessive due to poor credit control.

- *Cash and cash equivalents.* Supply chain projects and initiatives produce results that impact on this financial asset in the form of cost savings, efficiencies and waste reduction.

- *Property, plant and equipment.* Supply chain management is, in essence, the exercise of balancing profitability with the utilization of resources and company assets. Warehouses, truck fleets and equipment all combine here.

- *Accounts payable*. The way in which the company manages relations with its suppliers and compensates them – all Source processes, if we use the language of SCOR™ – is reflected here.

We are clearly starting to bring the financial and operational metrics together. We now have a firm basis on which to develop more innovative models. The next chapter looks at some of the creative thinking that has already stemmed from these principles, and we will find that the bridge between finance and operations is becoming ever stronger.

6

Mapping Operations with Finance

We now have a healthy list of operational and financial metrics with which to work.

Our purpose is to build a model that allows us to correlate these metrics, so that any activity measured with one set of metrics will immediately have a corresponding effect on the other. The first question we must ask is whether we should use statistics to map the correlations.

A number of papers and research studies show statistical connections between maturely deployed supply chain operations and quantified financial results. For instance, a paper published by Accenture and INSEAD states that there is a correlation between an organization's financial success and the depth and quality of its supply chain.[1] By cross-tabulating the companies studied in the supply chain and financial performance categories the researchers found a very high degree of consistency, with supply chain leaders showing a higher-than-expected probability of also being financial leaders and vice versa. The pattern that emerged strongly suggests a direct relationship between the supply chain and financial performance.

Although statistical results provide mathematical and quantitative support for the correlations between operational and financial performance, in my frequent interactions with end-users I find that the common view is that, as long as they derive from a consensus-based approach and are reviewed by peers, even more qualitative and less mathematically elegant relations suffice as the foundation of a new paradigm for measuring performance. The work

---

1   R.L. d'Avanzo, C.E. Starr and H. Von Lewinski, 'Supply Chain and the Bottom Line: A Critical Link', *Outlook*, February 2004, published on the Accenture website at: http://www.accenture.com/Global/Research_and_Insights/Outlook/By_Alphabet/SupplyLink.htm.

presented in this book stems from a decision not to use statistics but to accept that it is good enough to rely on consensus-based mapping to produce a table of the most likely dependencies between operational and financial performance indicators.

A number of applications in the business world show that it is acceptable to run a qualitative mapping process, supported by internal financial experts, and to immediately start linking operational decisions to financial performance. Many companies have developed sophisticated processes for this, and, once again, we might look to Strauss Elite and its implementation of the Control-and-Command Business Platform that delivers on-time analysis of relevant information to executives and managers at all levels, helping them to execute their tasks more efficiently. The company's system, and the Formula Builder it contains, provides a single formula that calculates all the final figures for the various interconnected business models.

Case Study: DHL Exel

Another example of internal mapping based on approved consensus versus a sophisticated statistical analysis comes from DHL Exel Supply Chain, one of the two logistics brands of the global market leader in international express, overland transport and air freight.

Figure 6.1 shows what DHL calls the company 'value lever' tree. This represents the CEO's long-term performance strategy for the company's supply chain, the goal of which is measured in terms of total return to shareholders (TRS) – the value generated by the company and the return expected by its shareholders.

To support the CEO's decision on what actions to take in order to achieve the expected return, the model breaks down the TRS value as the result of the difference between two components:

1. return on invested capital

2. weighted average cost of capital (WACC).

The first component quantifies how well the company generates cash flow relative to the capital it has invested in its business. The second component,

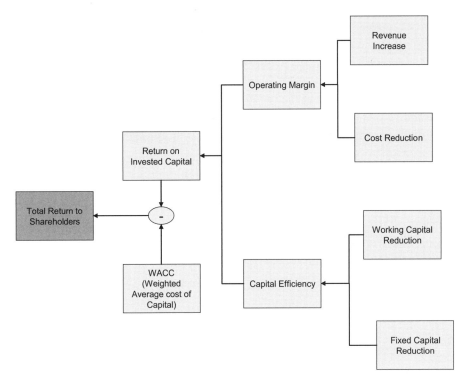

Figure 6.1   The value lever tree
Source: DHL Express.

WACC, should already be familiar. The formula that calculates the final value of TRS highlights the fact that when the return on capital is greater than the cost of capital – usually measured as the weighted average cost of capital – the company is creating value. When it is less than the cost of capital, value is destroyed.

The model goes beyond this initial correlation of factors to further break down the return on invested capital (ROIC) figure into its structural elements:

- operating margin

- capital efficiency.

Rather than providing a precise economic formula with which to calculate the financial ROIC, the model instead outlines the areas of intervention on which the CEO should focus to ensure that ROIC is under control and within the established boundaries. This will ultimately ensure the expected outcome of TRS. In fact, of the two elements required to calculate the result of the economic formula ROIC = (net profit) ÷ (invested capital), the DHL model suggests a capital efficiency indicator versus the exact value required for the formula denominator.

The model emphasizes that when a decision-maker's objective is to create value and return for company stakeholders, it becomes more relevant to assess the efficiency of a performance metric rather than quantifying its mere value. This is a vital part of the message this book wants to deliver.

The quest for efficiency requires that we identify those actions that lead us to achieve our desired result. 'Actions' is the key word – the operational decisions that lead directly to a change in financial performance. In the DHL model, the resulting performance is measured by capital efficiency, and the operational actions are the 'children' that branch out from the capital efficiency box:

- working capital reduction

- fixed capital reduction.

Once again, the model does not require the calculation of one-off metrics. Instead, it requires the evaluation of improvement actions on two key factors that heavily contribute to the efficiency of their capital efficiency 'parent'.

Similar in nature is the decomposition of the other component of ROIC: operating margin. The exact calculation of this factor, also known as net operating profit after taxes (NOPAT), results, in its simplified form, from the difference between revenue, operating costs (COGS plus SG&A costs) and tax expense. In the DHL model, we have, instead, the breakdown of two components which are, by their nature, actionable items:

- Increase revenue

- Reduce costs.

The message that consistently emerges from the model directs the executive manager to focus on actionable items that positively affect the final TRS. Although it may seem flimsy, this is initial evidence that managers can and often want to take decisions with only qualitative support rather than a more mathematical model.

In Figure 6.2 we see the final compilation of the DHL model, with a deep drill down on to the actionable items that enable a company to accomplish its targeted improvements. This is the practical evidence of it closing the gap between financial performance, expressed by TRS, and operational decisions listed on the right as 'leaves' on what DHL calls the 'value tree'. These actions represent the translation of metrics into operational indications on how to achieve the targeted results.

An increase in revenue, which contributes to the operating margin figure, is accomplished through actions aimed at generating revenue uplift. The 'how to' indications are focused on improving product availability through pooled stock. This is a practice that suggests keeping stock in a centralized location and making it available via a system that provides visibility of stock locations and item availability. It is also known as risk pooling, which is an important concept in supply chain management. Risk pooling suggests that demand variability is reduced if one aggregates demand across locations because, as we do so, it becomes more likely that high demand from one customer will be offset by low demand from another. This reduction in variability allows a decrease in safety stock and therefore reduces average inventory. As in the example of a centralized distribution system, the warehouse serves all customers, which leads to a reduction in variability measured by either the standard deviation or the coefficient of variation. Increased responsiveness and greater visibility of supply are additional actionable items on which the operations people at DHL will concentrate.

Another set of 'leaves' on the value tree represents the actions needed to reduce costs. Supply chain operators must focus on improving margins, rationalizing network costs, leveraging freight procurement, working on labour arbitrage and incurring lower airfreight costs. Of course, each action can be broken down into sub-tasks with more granular detail. What counts most in this case is that the path is indeed taking us from high-level financial performance targets towards more operational tasks expressed in the language of the people responsible for performing those tasks. The same comments apply to the other two branches of the value tree, directed at reducing working capital and fixed capital.

We see evidence – especially from these last two examples of families of actions – that the term 'operational' attributed to these actions must not only refer to operators on the materials handling side of the supply chain. The term covers all processes directly involving people in the supply chain whose activity

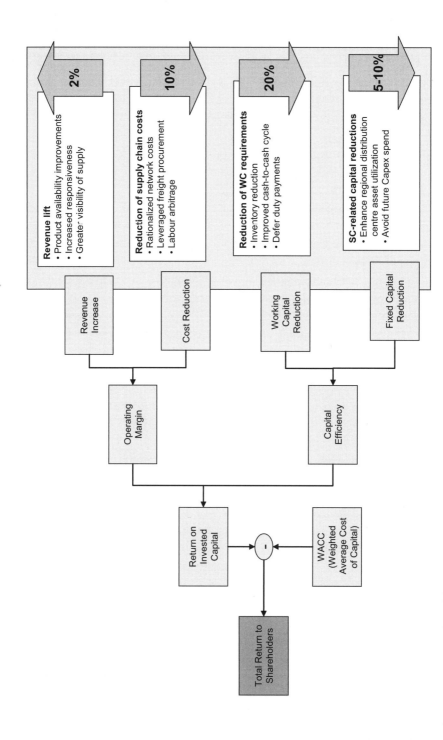

Figure 6.2   Actionable items in the DHL model
Source: DHL Express.

significantly impacts on final performance results. By this I mean all those involved in value-added activities that transform inputs into outputs and which are aligned with market opportunities for optimal enterprise performance.

We have a clear indication of this when reading, in Figure 6.2, 'Improved cash-to-cash cycle', 'Avoid future Capex spend' or 'Defer duty payments' among the operational actions. These tasks are related more to the daily activities of resources working in the controlling units or in the purchasing department. What is important, once again, is that a true integration among functional units is made possible not through a generic intention to collaborate simply because it makes sense to do so, but, rather, by tasking each unit with specific duties that all concur to generate a harmonized final performance.

In order to build a consistent and practical model, DHL managers have also established target levels for each of the operational action families. For instance, a 2 per cent increase is expected from the 'revenue lift' operations, while the 'reduction of working capital requirements' is targeted at almost 20 per cent. Once again, operational actions are directed towards achieving operational results that translate into improved financial performance.

This is made evident in an example presented by DHL during the 2006 European Executive Retreat of the Supply Chain Council (see Figure 6.3). The ability to translate operational actions into financial performance allowed DHL Exel to quantify the direct impact of supply chain improvements on firm value. In fact, in the mathematical example a measured profit value of €200 with a profit per earning ratio of 15 corresponds to a market capitalization of €3000. It is relatively straightforward to assess the impact of the supply chain costs as a percentage of a company's revenue. Benchmark data sources can also help identify such a value. A figure of 8 per cent of supply chain costs on revenue is fairly likely in most industries, yet here it is in the high quartile given the nature of DHL's business, which is asset-intensive and relies heavily on supply chain performance. In other industries the ratio is likely to be within the 4–6 per cent range.

By using the model and quantifying the likely results of the improvement actions shown in the leaves of the value tree, the numbers in the example show a beneficial return of 5 per cent in terms of cost reduction. This means that only one of the several families of operational actions – perhaps the easiest to quantify – has been considered. This reduction in supply chain costs equals an uplift of €20 in profit increase, which corresponds to an increased market capitalization from €3000 to €3300. The bottom line is that a 5 per cent reduction in supply

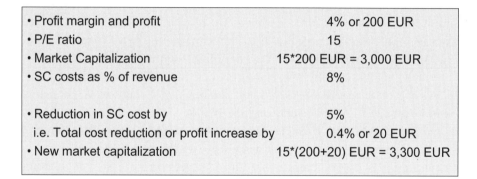

• Profit margin and profit	4% or 200 EUR
• P/E ratio	15
• Market Capitalization	15*200 EUR = 3,000 EUR
• SC costs as % of revenue	8%
• Reduction in SC cost by	5%
i.e. Total cost reduction or profit increase by	0.4% or 20 EUR
• New market capitalization	15*(200+20) EUR = 3,300 EUR

Figure 6.3   Estimated results
Source: DHL Express.

chain costs achieved by implementing one or more of the operational actions listed in the model results in a 10 per cent increase in market capitalization.

Bridging the divide between supply chain actions and corporate financial performance is, therefore, evidently possible. Borrowing the words of Oliver Landgraf, head of business development at DHL, we can say that the whole purpose of this exercise was for the company to 'use the appropriate language and measurement to communicate the value of supply chain'.[2]

Case Study: CHEP

Another useful example of a model built to bridge operational decisions with financial performance is provided by CHEP, an international pallet and container pooling company that supplies customers with pallets and reusable containers through a large network of depots. Pallet and container pooling is the shared use of standard pallets and containers by multiple customers. The company is part of the worldwide CHEP organization, which operates in more than 30 countries on six continents and controls more than 122 million pallets and 15 million containers.

In Figure 6.4 we see the model adopted by CHEP, which very closely resembles the one used by DHL. Instead of total return to shareholders (TRC) we have here business value added (BVA). This item quantifies the value generated by the company and is broken down into its two major components: NOPAT and capital charge. Using the same logic of deconstructing the tree into

---

2   Author's notes following a presentation by Oliver Landgraf.

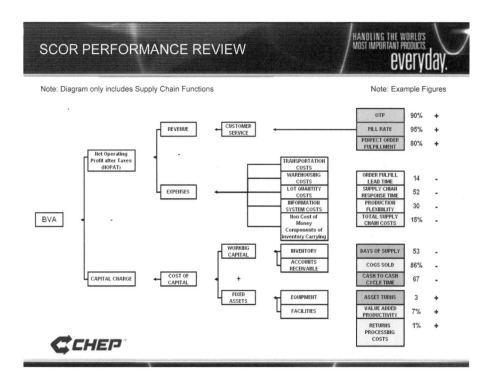

Figure 6.4   The CHEP model
Source: CHEP.

its constituent branches brings us to revenue and expenses as the 'children' of
the NOPAT branch, while capital charge is characterized by cost of capital.

If we move one layer to the right, climbing to the higher branches of
the tree, revenue is further decomposed into a more relevant contributor –
customer service. Expenses consist of the set of costs related to transportation,
warehousing, lot quantity, information system and the cost components of
inventory carrying costs. A set of such components is:

- storage

- handling

- obsolescence

- damage

- administrative

- loss (for example, pilferage).

These figures could also be defined as non-interest bearing liabilities associated with inventory carrying costs. Their purpose is to reiterate the operational nature of the model. The cost of capital is naturally obtained by the sum of working capital and fixed assets, respectively decomposed into inventory plus accounts receivable, and into equipment and facilities.

It is evident that the elements from which this kind of value tree are constructed are all pertinent to the nature of CHEP's business. The presence of transportation and lot quantity costs, the charge of inventory carrying costs and the quantification of equipment and facilities are all there to underline the asset-intensive nature of an international pallet and container pooling company.

We can already see from the CHEP model that more precise research is required to calculate the formulae that lead to the financial results. In fact, the model also illustrates the numbers that result from the calculations. The intent to quantify the results through such a model is most probably intended to support the extensive development of 'what-if' scenarios. Whereas the DHL model delves into more operational characteristics, the CHEP model applies to a calculation tool that gives a final figure for the total business value generated by the company.

The alignment of the CHEP model with the DHL model – in building a bridge between financial performance and operational decisions – can be seen in the 'leaves' at the far right of this value tree. Where the DHL model showed tasks that would lead the company towards achieving the intended results, the CHEP model instead highlights the SCOR™ metrics as the means of bridging the financial results so far calculated with actionable items. CHEP uses a more rigorous approach to calculating the impact of financial performance and operational decisions. It is therefore interesting to see that the CHEP model uses the SCOR™ metrics to generate the last-mile connection.

The acceptance of the SCOR™ metrics as a *de facto* standard makes them a credible support for the rigour of the model. Not only has the SCOR™ model provided a best practice and an unbiased means by which to calculate value, but it also presents a number of connections between these same performance metrics and the practices successfully adopted by the members of the Supply Chain Council community to close eventual measured performance gaps.

It is important to emphasize the nature of the practices that are developed, tested and promoted directly by the practitioners. In the Supply Chain Council there are no 'super–guru' consultants who decide what should or should not be in the model. The practitioners themselves collaborate to ensure that their experience and successfully adopted practices become a methodology that can be shared with other members.

Comparing CHEP with DHL

A superficial view of both DHL and CHEP models highlights their similarity in nature and structure, in that the bridge between financial performance and operational supply chain decisions is represented by a breakdown of constituent components, which creates a natural correlation between elements that seem irreconcilably different.

The term 'value tree', used by DHL, neatly expresses the topology of the model that graphically represents the parent–child correlations as branches of a tree. The resulting image very closely resembles another breakdown structure that is already very well known by supply chain experts – the bill of materials (BOM). A BOM basically consists of a list of parts and is essential to the design and manufacture of any product. It often contains hierarchical information, with the master, or top–level, BOM describing a list of components and sub-assemblies. This increasing level of detail continues for all sub-assemblies until the BOM reaches its constituent parts.

A BOM is often graphically represented as an upside-down tree structure. The finished product sits at the roots of the tree, while the branches represent the parent–child relations between the finished product and its components at increasing levels of detail.

In Figure 6.5, the per-unit quantities are also represented to allow immediate calculation of the totals required for volume productions. From this graphical model we are able to derive the product structure and the quantities involved in its production.

If we take the bill of materials tree and rotate it 90° to the left we immediately recognize the structure of the value tree. Just as the supply chain manager recognizes the structure of a bill of materials and knows how to read it and use it, the chief financial officer understands the structure of a value tree. That

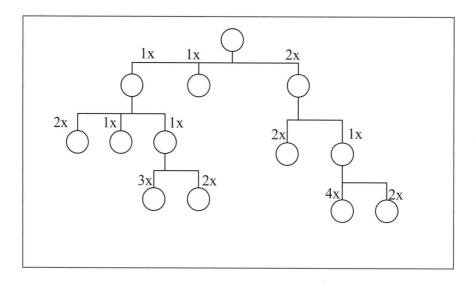

Figure 6.5   A bill of materials

is why I like to refer to the tree structure of both the DHL and CHEP models as the chief financial officer's bill of materials – or, to simplify, the CFO's BOM.

The CFO's Bill of Materials

The tree structures used by DHL-Exel and CHEP are only two examples of what any financial manager would use to simulate and assess the creation of corporate value. Furthermore, this is not a new methodology, as the first examples of value tree models date back to the beginning of the twentieth century. In an industry characterized by vertical integration and heavy investments in both physical plants and inventories, the financial experts at DuPont developed a formula that enabled productivity and asset utilization to be measured in the same equation. This formula is known as the DuPont formula, the DuPont identity or DuPont analysis. It represented the first significant step in focusing on supply chain execution.

The formula is an expression that breaks return on investment (ROI) into two major parts:

1.   operating efficiency (measured by net margin)

2.   asset use efficiency (measured by asset turnover).

When we develop it further, we derive formula 6.1:

ROI = (net profit/sales) × (sales/assets) = (net margin) × (asset turnover)

Analysis of the formula shows that it is well suited to measuring an organization's progress towards the goal of balancing net margin (profitability) with asset utilization. This is made clearer in Figure 6.6.

Here, net margin and asset turnover are inversely proportional. The supply chain manager therefore has more than one lever with which to influence ROI. It would be of great help to supply chain managers to identify which of the levers to pull in order to gain the best result from the operations for which they are responsible. Common practice suggests that they will have more success if they focus on company assets. Practices and technologies require careful allocation of company assets if prescribed objectives are to be attained.

Cash, equipment, buildings and land are all examples of assets, and it seems obvious how good supply chain practices can positively affect their use. Cash can be influenced by cautious management of inventory resources, be they raw materials, work in progress or finished goods. All these elements of inventory tie up a company's cash in two ways: the cash required to buy material from the

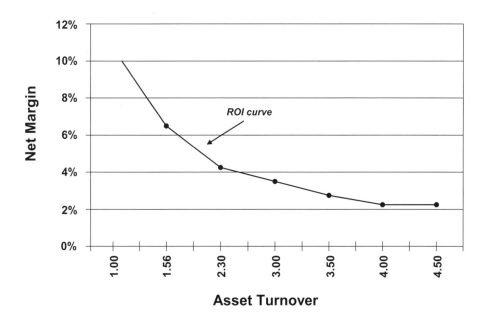

Figure 6.6   Net margin and asset turnover

suppliers, and cash allocated to company resources spent on transforming the material into work in progress as semi-finished or finished goods.

Equipment is another asset directly under the supply chain manager's control. Practices such as 'capable to promise' directly relate to the manager's ability to plan and schedule the use of the company apparatus and tools in line with the process of transforming goods. 'Capable to promise' involves a time-phased functionality, used by some manufacturing systems, which checks component availability far down the supply chain, as well as available materials and machine and resource capacity, to determine whether a particular product can be delivered by a specific date. Basically, with a 'capable to promise' feature, order-takers can quickly work out whether they can meet the customer's requested date, based on available capacity and material. If the requested date cannot be met, 'capable to promise' offers the earliest date that can realistically be promised and gives alternative delivery options, such as split orders. When the customer agrees the order, 'capable to promise' automatically generates any new jobs or job quantity changes.

Of course, a company such as a retailer that is less focused on the physical transformation of goods can still leverage the use of company equipment. Trucks, forklifts, warehouse hardware, automatic palletizers, barcode readers, wireless devices, software tools and investments in automated applications are all part of the assets under the control of supply chain managers and their teams.

Buildings and land are also measures of the supply chain manager's ability to do more with less. As he focuses on properly sizing the number of warehouses, distribution centres and stocking units to keep in the supply–distribution network, he can also be responsible for managing the production and process layout, suggesting how to use less space to keep stocks, run operations and reduce the space between machines in production cells. These are all aspects of building and land that can be converted as supply chain managers seek to either save unutilized space or fill the available space for which they have already paid.

So far, we have seen many reasons why a supply chain manager should concentrate on asset turnover to generate maximum return. This is further supported by the fact that the other component of the ROI equation, net margin, is hardly in the hands of the supply chain manager alone. As the DuPont chart depicted in Figure 6.7 (p. 156) shows, net margin is the result of sales minus expenses. Given that expenses is the combination of COGS and SG&A costs, it becomes apparent that the supply chain manager has fewer anchor points from which to implement actions for improvement. COGS quantifies the cost of producing a product or service to be sold to the market: it represents the total costs of acquiring raw materials and turning them into finished goods. It generally has three main components: direct labour, direct materials and manufacturing overhead. Direct labour covers the cost of all labour, such as assembly-line workers, employed directly in the manufacture of goods, as opposed to support functions like maintenance. Manufacturing overhead includes all costs necessary for the production of goods but not tied to specific goods. This includes such items as indirect labour, indirect materials, property taxes, insurance, heat and light.

The only other way to raise the value of net margin is by increasing the value of sales – in other words, by increasing the price of final goods. Some supply chain management practices can indeed help achieve this objective. Ensuring a perfect response time or a superior quality of product and service delivery against a premium for specific customer segments, or for specific product brands, makes it possible to maintain relatively high prices that buyers are still willing to pay. Adaptability through a more flexible supply chain is also an attribute that enables the vendor to offer customized solutions at a higher price than the competition, maintaining a positive differential between the sustained costs and the retail price of goods sold.

Nevertheless, supply chain efforts can push to a point, but no further. Profitability margins are tied to many variables independent of supply chain management's ability to generate additional revenue. For instance, as soon as sales and marketing promote discounts and special offers in line with strategies to increase the volumes of sales or to cut out a competitor's product from a specific market segment, the supply chain is pulled back into cost-cutting endeavours – the expenses side of the equation.

Clearly, the levers that supply chain managers can pull to reduce the expenses figure are limited in number. Many decisions, such as cost of labour or cost of purchased goods, reside in other people's hands. Taxes, insurance, heat and light are variables that the supply chain executive can help control, but virtuous supply chain activities can only exploit them for a small fraction of their total value.

The final consequence of this analysis – that a supply chain manager's efforts can be more effectively applied to improve the asset turnover component of the ROI (formula 6.1) – is further supported by running some numbers:

Formula 6.1 reads that:

$$ROI = (net\ margin) \times (asset\ turnover)$$

If we add some numerical values to this equation we might assume that ROI equals 7.6 per cent, which is perfectly likely; we could also assign values of 4.9 per cent and 1.56 per cent to net margin and asset turnover respectively. The formula then becomes:

$$7.6\% = 4.9\% \times 1.56$$

If the objective is to increase ROI from 7.6 per cent to, say, 10 per cent, there are two ways of doing so. First, we could increase net margin while maintaining the same value for asset turnover. Alternatively, we could increase asset turnover while keeping the same net margin value.

For the first scenario, net margin must increase by 30.6 per cent to reach 6.4 per cent if ROI is to top the expected 10 per cent:

$$10\% = 6.4\%\ (+ 30.6\%) \times 1.56$$

When asset turnover changes, the increase required is far smaller – only one third of the increase required for net margin in the previous example. A 23.5 per cent increase in asset turnover is sufficient to get to an ROI of 10 per cent:

$$10\% = 4.9\% \times 2.04\ (+ 23.5\%)$$

Smaller increases in asset turnover tend to produce a higher ROI value.

Beyond the DuPont Formula

Traditionally, supply chain management processes and techniques balance supply and demand. They anticipate customer demand via sophisticated forecasting mechanisms and fulfil it with available capacity of supply resources such as material, equipment and labour. Now, a new scenario characterized by globalized networks requires a balancing act between profitability – the lowering of total costs – and utilization of assets, which represents the overall efficiency of the supply chain. In other words, the unrelenting desire to slash costs by removing all kinds of waste must be counterbalanced with the efficient utilization of company assets – equipment, capital, inventories – that build the company's balance sheet.

Isolating variables of net income and asset utilization can be done by multiplying the quotient of the return on sales ratio (net profit/sales) with that of the total asset turnover ratio (sales/assets). This calculation provides strong support to executives who have always been aware of the need to align balance sheet and income statement performance. Some simple maths makes the point. In the DuPont formula the denominator in the net margin equation and numerator in the asset turnover equation are the same – net sales. Basic algebra suggests that this variable cancels itself out, leaving a new equation that reads:

$$\text{ROI} = (\text{net profit} \div \text{sales}) \times (\text{sales} \div \text{assets}) = (\text{net profit} \div \text{assets})$$

From this, the manager is encouraged to break down the components of each equation in an attempt to trace financial results back to operating tactics. This breakdown also allows the manager to identify the root causes of problems and systematically eliminate them.

One of the most powerful contributions made by the DuPont model becomes clearer when we see it represented graphically, as in Figure 6.7. First, the picture helps us understand the financial links that exist between operational challenges and poor financial performance. In fact, the primary indicators of financial performance – net profit margin and total asset turnover – are decomposed into elements that are tightly related to activities that lead to operational excellence.

Net profit derives from the difference between sales and expenses. The sales figure is closely linked to supply chain operations, as we have already seen. It quantifies an organization's ability to fulfil customer expectations through effective distribution and delivery services. By improving these processes the organization is able to expand into new markets and open up new channels for both new and existing products. All this leads to increased sales volumes.

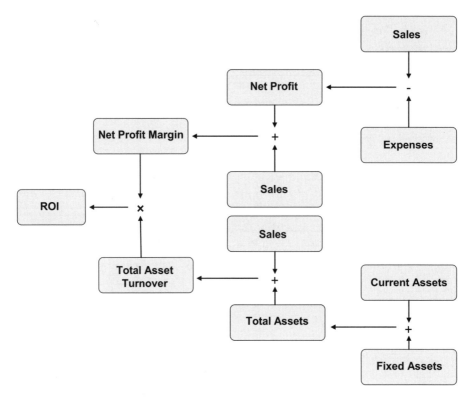

Figure 6.7   The DuPont model

As for expenses, we have already analysed this figure when we referred to COGS and SG&A. We can effectively say that these two expense factors mainly contribute to reducing the contribution of sales to the overall value of the company profit, and I have shown what a supply chain manager can and should do to reduce their negative effects.

The connection between financial performance and operational tactics is also evident when we look at total assets. When broken down, its components – current assets and fixed assets – draw the supply chain manager's attention, as he will have a number of tools readily available to increase the efficiency in these areas. From a longer-term perspective, better asset utilization and capacity management can free up investment in capital assets. Better alignment of demand with supply sources reduces the need for additional investment in fixed assets and frees up capital for other strategic initiatives.

As previously seen, the (sales ÷ assets) component of the ROI formula suggests that asset turnover has a higher impact on ROI. In fact, the (net profit ÷

sales) component can increase by increasing the numerator – net profit. Now, it is extremely difficult to operate by increasing this factor unless the company operates in a purely monopolistic environment with almost free control on prices.

The other important aspect of the DuPont chart is that it simultaneously represents elements of both the balance sheet and income statement. In fact, net profit margin and all its correlated branches are part of the income statement report. So, too, are sales and expenses and their related elements COGS and SG&A, expressing the company's ability to achieve profitability, particularly through those operations that sit firmly within the domain of supply chain management. The lower part of Figure 6.7 represents items whose values can be extracted from the balance sheet, in which current assets and fixed assets are both important elements.

Overall, because it simultaneously focuses on both profit and capital, the DuPont model provides a simple and useful operating measure to account for the many income statement and balance sheet trade-offs involved in creating value.

The ramifications of the column furthest to the right of the CFO's BOM represent the connections, or adapters, in relation to the operational activities that affect them. Supply chain managers can, therefore, identify those actions and practices they can perform to affect either the income statement portion of the model – the net margin value of the ROI formula – or its balance sheet portion, where it is mainly aimed at improving asset turnover. It is not, of course, the supply chain manager's responsibility to choose which portion of the ROI formula to attack. This is a strategic decision that must be taken at board level.

There is no doubt, however, that supply chain managers can raise their standing among the decision-makers by improving the quality of their interaction with board executives. They can do so by clearly explaining the activities that constitute improvement actions in the supply chain in terms of their effects on income statement and balance sheet.

From the DuPont to the EVA Model

In measuring corporate performance, executives have come to embrace a concept known as economic value added (EVA), which is a registered trademark of Stern Stewart & Co. Put simply, EVA is calculated by subtracting from NOPAT a charge for the capital used to produce profits. It follows that EVA can be improved by generating more profits with the same capital – including inventory, accounts receivable, cash, plant and equipment – or by producing the same level of profits using fewer capital resources. The power of EVA is that it focuses the attention of decision-makers on those things that increase value to shareholders: increasing sales, reducing costs and better managing assets.

In Figure 6.8 we see an EVA calculation for a fictitious firm, Acme Company.

The first calculation we see in Figure 6.8 is Acme's income statement. Acme has sales of €$1 million and an average cost of sales of 50 per cent. The firm has general and administrative (SG&A) expenses of €400 000, which remain relatively fixed, and its tax rate is 40 per cent. These figures yield a net operating profit after taxes (NOPAT) of €60 000. Acme's income statement, however, does not tell the whole story. To generate US$1 million of sales, the company employs €500 000 of capital from shareholder equity or lenders, or both. Assuming a 10 per cent cost of capital, Acme must generate €50 000 to shareholders and lenders as a fair return. Acme's EVA as a corporation is €10 000, meaning that the company generated €10 000 in value after paying investors and creditors for the use of their capital. If EVA were negative, it would mean that the company had destroyed value, as it would be generating a less than adequate ROI.

Acme Company		
Sales	€1,000,000	
Less cost of sales (COGS)	(500,000)	
Less general and administrative expenses (SG&A)	(400,000)	
Net operating profit before taxes		100,000
Less taxes @ 40%		(40,000)
Net Operating Profit After Taxes (NOPAT)		€60,000
Less Capital Charge		
Capital	500,000	
Cost of Capital	10%	
Capital Charge		(50,000)
Economic Profit (EVA)		€10,000

Figure 6.8   EVA in action

Although calculating EVA seems relatively simple, computing the EVA for a real corporation can require several adjustments before NOPAT can be derived from the income statement and capital from the balance sheet. This is because, according to generally accepted accounting principles (GAAP), net profit contains many assumptions that cause it to differ from the actual amount of cash left at year-end. According to Stern Stewart, turning standard financials into forms that can be used to calculate EVA requires adjustments for non-cash expenses to be made to earnings and balance sheet accounts. Furthermore, the weighted average cost of debt and equity capital must be calculated, and material changes in the mix of various forms of debt and equity can affect the cost of capital.

The formula for calculating cost of capital is not simple, but it is interesting to learn how it works. I have previously outlined the importance of cost of capital in a buyer–supplier relationship in modern, globalized supply chains, and the decisive financial factor banks use to decide how to finance suppliers from emerging markets is to arbitrage between the value of the cost of capital of these potential new customers and the cost of capital of their customer companies, the buyers. A supply chain manager must therefore be able to understand the mechanics behind these evaluations to assist their financial colleagues in negotiating with banks over possible funding solutions that will support suppliers' ability to remain financially viable and focus on serving the company to the highest standard.

The negative repercussions of a financially stressed supplier on the buyer's overall profitability are not always evident, but they do exist. If a supplier suffers due to a lack of funding it will be forced to borrow capital at a higher interest rate from investors who will inevitably expect a higher return, given the riskier nature of the investment. A financially stressed company is not exactly a safe place to put your money. The higher cost of money that the supplier must bear will somehow impact on the price of the goods sold to the customer. It may come in the form of increased prices for purchased goods, as often happens when a supplier provides a strategic and indispensable product to its customer, who will find a price increase still acceptable. Alternatively, it may manifest in a more subtle and dangerous way, with suppliers trying to make savings by cutting expenses wherever they can. As a result they may cut their procedures for ensuring the quality of delivered goods or services to a contractual minimum, which has the downside for the buyer of increased SG&A costs from controlling the goods from those suppliers and from running additional repairs and checks during the production phase. They will also, no doubt, have to respond to more complaints from their customers.

All this must be clear to a supply chain manager if he is to take the proper countermeasures and work with his financial counterparts to ensure sustainable growth through a close, virtuous cooperation with the supplier base.

Calculating the Cost of Capital

Cost of capital is better known in financial jargon as weighted average cost of capital (WACC), which we have already encountered. In mathematical terms, WACC is derived from Formula 6.2:

$$WACC = [\% \text{ debt} \times K_D \times (1 - t)] + [\% \text{ equity} \times K_E]$$

It is worth looking closely at what each factor in this formula means to a supply chain manager. The terms in the formula are defined as follows:

% debt = % debt financing

K_D = cost of debt

$(1 - t)$ = 100% – % marginal tax rate (t)

% equity = % equity financing

K_E = cost of equity

Some of these need further clarification. % debt financing represents the portion of the total financing value available to the company that is sourced mainly through loans from banks. K_D is the cost of the money lent by the bank, and its value is published daily in financial papers, is publicly traded and is governed by market dynamics.

The $(1 - t)$ factor reflects in the purely operational nature of the calculation of the cost of capital. As a perfectly legitimate and institutionalized financial practice, companies use the financing debt they have negotiated with banks to leverage a tax-exemption instrument known as 'tax shield'. This instrument is well known to anyone who has an active mortgage with a bank. Generally the portion of the mortgage capital interests paid to the bank can be deducted from the personal income profile, resulting in a lower amount of personal income tax payable to the state. The same principle inspires companies to lower the total value of gross income – known as earnings before income taxes (EBIT) – in order to reduce their tax burden. This is, however, a purely financial technique to which there is no contribution from the operational execution of the supply chain. Calculation of WACC from a supply chain perspective must abstract from purely financial operations such as lease, investment and sale of real estate. And this is made possible through the (1 – t) factor.

The importance of debt must be explained further if we are to appreciate the contribution of supply chain operations to the decision-making process. When a company grows, it typically needs to invest in new assets – plant, equipment and warehouses. To finance this expansion it could issue new stock or incur debt. To the extent a company can increase its asset base though debt financing, it increases its leverage. Debt enjoys several advantages over equity. For one, it is a cheaper source of capital and it also brings certain tax advantages. Also, unlike equity, maximizing debt does not dilute ownership, so any growth provides more return to the existing owners.

Debt financing does not come without risk, however, because interest charges are incurred and must be paid before distributions to shareholders. Consequently, management may not want to maximize financial leverage, and most companies will have a debt capacity threshold. This is determined by the point at which lenders refuse additional credit and there is too little cash to pay the interest charges.

Supply chain management decisions cannot help determine which financial levers to pull, but they can give an organization more confidence in its operations, which in turn will give it greater flexibility when making financial decisions. Operational decisions can provide visibility into earnings, which may allow the company to take on more interest risk. Improved operations resulting from supply chain practices and technologies can also generate additional cash flow to pay off debt, while a higher quality of earnings enables organizations to negotiate better interest rates or receive a better bond rating. Together, these factors lower the cost of debt.

The decision over whether to focus more on debt or equity financing is represented in formula 6.2 by the % equity factor. This value complements the % debt figure to account for all of a company's financing decisions. K_E quantifies the cost of financing through equity and requires more detailed examination.

Figure 6.9 shows a graphical representation of formula 6.3 (below) which is used to calculate the value of K_E:

$$K_E = \text{(risk-free rate)} + \text{(beta} \times \text{equity risk premium)}$$

This is the formula for a straight line, originating from the rate of a risk-free investment such as a 20-year Treasury bond. This is a safe investment because it is backed by the government, which is considered unlikely to default on its loans, and for that reason it is used as reference point by which to benchmark the interest calculations for any other equity instrument.

The independent variable of the equation is equity risk premium, which relates to the nature of the investment and quantifies the return expected by investors who have put their money into a given asset. This variable relates to a decision process that can be easily explained. If I decide to invest my money in a utility company I will expect a higher return than if I keep it tied up in a 20-year Treasury bond. The return should certainly be higher if my money goes to an average for-profit company, such as a retailer or an automotive company.

The more we move to the right of the horizontal axis, the riskier the investment. The results we should expect from a computer manufacturer

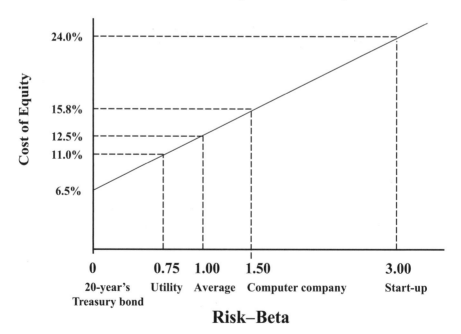

Figure 6.9   Calculating K_E

should be higher than from companies in preceding sectors and an investment in a start-up company must promise even better results to attract capital, which is otherwise parked in safer investments. The slope of the line is determined by the beta factor, which is the most important element in the whole calculation of WACC. Beta, also known as the 'beta coefficient' or 'volatility factor', quantifies the volatility of the investment in relation to the rest of the market.

A company's beta is calculated using regression analysis. It measures the part of the asset's statistical variance that cannot be mitigated by the diversification provided by a portfolio of many risky assets, because it is correlated with the return of the other assets that are in the portfolio. Investments tend to be correlated, particularly within a specific industry. This correlated risk, measured by beta, is what creates almost all of the risk in a diversified portfolio.

Figure 6.10 shows a set of data on beta for different industry sectors. A beta of 1 indicates that a security's price tends to move with the market. A beta greater than 1 indicates that a security's price tends to be more volatile than the market, and a beta less than 1 means that it tends to be less volatile than the market.

Many utility stocks have a beta of less than 1, while many hi-tech stocks listed on NASDAQ have a beta greater than 1. Roughly speaking, a security with a beta of 1.5 will move, on average, 1.5 times more than the market return.

We could discuss beta in great detail, as it is a complex factor to study, but it suffices to say that, all things being equal, the higher a company's beta, the higher its cost of capital discount rate. The higher the discount rate, the lower the present value placed on the company's future cash flows, which is another way of looking at the cost of capital. In short, beta can have an impact on a company's share valuation.

The final element of formula 6.2 is equity risk premium which measures the excess return that an individual stock or the overall stock market provides over a risk-free rate. This excess return compensates investors for taking on the relatively higher risk of the equity market. The size of the premium will vary in line with the changing risks of a particular stock or of the stock market as a whole. High-risk investments are compensated with a higher premium. The reason for this premium stems from the risk–return trade-off, in which a higher rate of return is required to entice investors to take on riskier investments.

Industry Name	Total Beta (Unlevered)
Aerospace/Defense	1.99
Auto and Truck	1.15
Auto Parts	1.93
Bank	0.89
Beverage (Soft Drink)	1.28
Cement and Aggregates	1.81
Chemical (Basic)	1.69
Computer Software/Svcs	6.04
Electronics	4.37
Food Processing	1.51
Healthcare Information	3.18
Homebuilding	1.32
Insurance (Life)	1.57
Machinery	2.03
Maritime	1.31
Medical Services	2.89
Metal Fabricating	2.44
Office Equip/Supplies	1.87
Packaging and Container	1.28
Paper/Forest Products	1.23
Petroleum (Producing)	2.49
Pharmacy Services	1.88
Retail Store	1.99
Semiconductor	6.35
Steel (General)	2.87
Telecom. Services	2.89
Trucking	1.69
Wireless Networking	5.90

Figure 6.10   Beta by industry sector

Source: http://pages.stern.nyu.edu/~adamodar/New_Home_Page/data.html.

To summarize, WACC averages the two components of cost of capital: capital from debt (loans from banks) and capital from equity. This is an important point, as it highlights the more financial nature of EVA and demonstrates that the supply chain manager needs to become familiar with terms such as risk and volatility of investments and assets. There is a large body of research on risk management in supply chains, and many research documents provide frameworks for assessing a company's propensity for, or aversion to, risk. The EVA formula quantifies the elements that contribute to the overall calculation of the value generated by the company in face of market volatility and risk factors. It can also be also graphically represented as a breakdown tree just like DuPont model, as we can see in the example illustrated in Figure 6.11.

The Difference between the DuPont and EVA models

The DuPont model focuses mainly on operational profitability and asset utilization. It is very much oriented towards operational excellence. Conversely, EVA focuses more on cost of capital and the value created for shareholders. The main difference between the two models is in the way in which they consider assets.

The DuPont formula refers to the ROI of assets, with the objective of finding a sustainable balance between the utilization of these assets and the company's

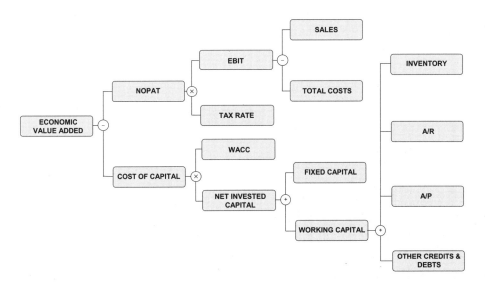

Figure 6.11   The EVA tree

profitability. It prioritizes the operational excellence of the supply chain. EVA, on the other hand, places greater emphasis on the impact these assets have on value. The company must reap the benefits from its available capital both by improving operational excellence, measured by the NOPAT line of correlations, and by ensuring that the value obtained, measured as economic profit, is higher in the eyes of the investors than the return from lower-risk investments. The critical decision factor is measured in terms of cost of capital.

The DuPont model provides another early step in closing the gap between supply chain managers and the finance directors. The existing misalignment between cost reduction, operational excellence and value creation defines what we can call the internal gap – 'internal' because it is generated within the company. The internal gap is important because a company must first enable internal collaboration before exposing itself to partnerships in the open market.

The importance of internal collaboration is made very clear if we consider e-business and e-commerce strategies, which serve as a practical example. Collaborating with the aim of maximizing value for the end-user is the only way a company in this sector can stay competitive. At the same time, however, many companies are realizing that vertical integration in order to take control of the value chain through mergers and acquisitions is not necessarily the best approach. Through network supply chains with good e-business solutions, companies can find the best parties to run their value chain processes and still remain sufficiently flexible to meet changing market demands.

Many companies are now taking a step back to review their own internal processes, as well as those of their business partners. Most companies are still operating with silo structures, in which product development, procurement, manufacturing, sales and logistics focus solely on their own processes, independently of their colleagues in other departments. In the ERP age (1980s–1990s) – when Forbes Global 2000 organizations[3] began to invest in automated software solutions to manage their business in a more integrated way – many companies restructured to fit the applications they were implementing. This led to many sub-optimizations, but seldom to any collaboration between internal silos. Now this is all changing. Companies are looking at their own processes with a view to optimizing and aligning them more closely with business strategy before implementing applications to support that strategy. Having cleaned up their own houses, the most advanced companies are now investigating how they

---

3   The Forbes Global 2000 is a useful indicator to identify the leading companies in the world.

can implement process collaboration externally, including the use of e-business applications to increase profitability. Even though a small enterprise with a website can open a window to the world, this does not in itself imply that the Web has replaced the need for a well-defined export strategy, derived from market analysis and an assessment of consumers' tastes.

The trend is moving away from e-commerce investments that are intended to keep a business ahead of its competitors and towards solutions that focus on establishing and consolidating existing activities and operations. Indeed, where companies were once intent on blindly acquiring new clients, they are now increasingly shifting towards reinforcing the relationships with their existing customers, as well as with all the other constituents of their business – suppliers, intermediaries, retailers and employees. European managers agree that e-business is taking root in many industries at a more capillary level, involving not only sales and marketing departments, but also back-office, provisioning and logistics functions. Awareness is shifting from forecast-driven to demand-driven operations. Collaboration certainly accelerates trade cycles and improves time-to-market, enabling partners to better sustain joint business objectives. However, the need to realign the current portfolio of internal solutions will make seeking complete collaborative relationship with external parties less urgent.

The major business impact of this trend is that the roots of competitive advantage are being repositioned within internal organizational processes. The benefits of external collaborative commerce will follow.

Establishing internal collaboration is important for preparing the way for a stronger and more sustainable rapport with external supply chain constituents. Collaboration is based primarily on trust, and trust must be shared by both parties. Trust is built on common targets and on the belief that these targets can be reached through collaboration, with both parties willing to pursue a win–win objective. Common targets must first be identified and shared under a common agreement.

Sharing and agreement presuppose that both parties speak the same language when communicating options and decisions. The most important aspect of collaboration is therefore the common language that brings together each party's intentions and objectives. This common language also initiates a negotiation of intents that becomes a clear set of actions aiming at the same target. It is crucial to have confidence that the other party is an ally.

Trust must first and foremost be built internally between supply chain management and finance. In the triangle of the information–goods–funds flow discussed in Chapter 3, finance and the supply chain are closely linked in closing the funds–information loop.

Much of the value of the DuPont model is in the language it provides to bridge supply chain management and finance. EVA, on the other hand, is geared more towards closing the external gap between company investors, shareholders and the company's board. The supply chain manager can play a greater role; he can provide evidence of how the actions performed as part of the supply chain management operations, guided by the DuPont model correlations, can have a positive impact on the company's overall economic profit.

Formula 6.4 shows the approach taken by EVA:

$$EP = NOPAT - CoC \times capital$$

EVA is also referred to as return on invested capital (ROIC), which highlights the two components that a company must balance in order to generate value: the overall sources of capital that, when invested, produce value; and the need to balance debt with equity to reduce the total cost of capital.

Supply chain managers do not have to spend time doing the maths to calculate the value of their company's cost of capital. They can simply ask their financial directors the value they use in the budgeting process, or, as many companies do, retain specialist consultants to recalculate the cost of capital every two or three years.

The Advantage of EVA

If they do not take an EVA-based approach to investment analysis, decision-makers are likely to focus only on improving net profit without considering the significant benefit to shareholders that comes with improving asset turnover.

To shareholders, this is just as important, if not more so, than improving net profits. This is because, as a firm grows, it often becomes more difficult to manage its assets as effectively. For example, a small company may do a good job of managing inventory in a single distribution centre, but if it doubles its sales and adds a second distribution centre it may find it needs three times the inventory to support a twofold increase in sales volume. Furthermore, in many industries there are limited opportunities to increase profitability. Customers demanding lower prices, higher service levels and greater customization put downward pressure on profitability. With only limited capacity to raise prices, companies need to increase asset turnover in order to improve shareholder value. Therefore, the best way for companies to improve enterprise value is to focus on improving asset turnover as well as increasing sales volume. In other words, they need to use fewer resources to sell more products and services.

Even if EVA is not used to measure the performance of a company as a whole, it can still be used as a tool to evaluate investment decisions. In evaluating a specific investment, we only need to estimate the change in EVA that would result if management approves the capital investment. Therefore, we can make simple, but reasonable, assumptions about net profit and the cost of capital, and, as long as we are consistent in our assumptions, the impact of the proposed investment on EVA should tell us quite a bit about whether the investment adds to, or destroys, shareholder value.

Figure 6.12 shows the calculation of EVA for a proposed investment in a new sales forecasting system.

Change in EVA for New Sales Forecasting System		
Increase in sales (5% of current sales of $1 million)	€50,000	
Cost of sales for the increase in sales (50%)	(25,000)	
Less change in G&A expens (system support costs)	(20,000)	
Change in net operating profit before taxes	5,000	
Less taxes @ 40%	(2,000)	
Change in net operating profit after taxes (NOPAT)		3,000
Less capital charge		
Capital investment for new system	30,000	
Reduction in average inventory assets due to new system	(20,000)	
Cost of capital	10%	
Capital charge		(1,000)
Economic profit (EVA) from new system		€2,000

Figure 6.12   EVA for evaluating investment decisions

In this example, Acme Company has determined that the new system will provide the following tangible benefits:

- Increased sales from having the right products on hand to meet customer demand. Acme estimates a 5 per cent increase in sales, or €50 000.

- Reduced inventory levels from having less of the wrong product on hand. Acme estimates that the new system will allow a 20 per cent reduction in its average inventory level of €100 000 – a benefit of €20 000.

On the cost side, the new sales forecasting system will require:

- an initial capital investment of €30 000

- ongoing support costs of €20 000 per year.

We can see from Figure 6.12 that the new sales forecasting system will generate an EVA of €2000 in the first year. In this example, the new system has a powerful impact on inventory. The €20 000 reduction in inventory assets in the first year offsets much of the initial capital investment.

Admittedly, this illustration is highly simplified, showing the EVA calculation only for the first year. In practice, a new system would have a useful life of at least five years, and the EVA calculation should be repeated over the anticipated life of the system, which may be discounted to a net present value that equates the net present value of cash flow. Nevertheless the example is useful for pointing out how shareholder value can be created in two ways: increasing net profits through higher sales and reducing capital as a result of improving inventory asset turnover.

Having discussed the principles of EVA and the SCOR™ and DuPont models, we now have the platform on which I have constructed my own model which is outlined in the next chapter.

7

A New Way to Model the Value of the Supply Chain

By studying the DuPont and EVA models in Chapter 6 we have gone a long way towards proving the importance of finding a common language in which supply chain managers and finance directors can communicate. The models also give us an insight into the kind of relationships between operational and financial metrics from which we can start to build that language.

One important tool is provided by the way in which these models represent mathematical formulae in a graphical format that is accessible to supply chain managers and which can help them identify the key operations that generate corporate value. Furthermore, this format gives them the means by which they can communicate their findings to the key stakeholders in a way that ensures they will be understood.

Both models begin with a financial indicator – ROI in the case of the DuPont model and economic profit (or ROIC) in the EVA model. These indicators are part of the vocabulary of the finance department and are the reference values that bridge the company with the external world. They are terms that communicate the company's ability to generate value for the stakeholders who have provided it with the capital and assets it requires to sustain its operations in the market and build a strategy for the future. The models break down their initial indicator into components and sub-components, creating a cascade of correlated factors that translate the initial financial measure of corporate value into the 'leaves' of a value tree.

In both the DuPont and EVA models the elements of accounts payable, accounts receivable, property and equipment are at the furthest reaches of the tree, and these are the metrics that constitute the interfaces that plug supply chain management into finance. These outermost 'leaves' have a direct correlation to operational measures. The results of accounts receivable in the balance sheet correspond to delivery reliability, particularly in a managed distribution supply chain. Also, the amount of accounts receivable represents the balance due of invoices less payments and therefore quantifies the effect of poor/ good credit control. Similarly, accounts payable is a direct consequence of supplier relationship management, as well as forecast accuracy and reliability.

Despite the fact that this process of mapping financial results with operational practices is the most important element of added value in both the DuPont and EVA models, so far it has not been subject to thorough analysis by researchers. It is time for that to change, given that the door it opens up could lead to a very different way of viewing the supply chain and its importance in creating corporate value and defining strategy.

Stepping through the Door

Now that we have explored the many ways in which companies are measuring their supply chains, and the innovative thinking that is inspired by their experiences of doing so, we have come to the end of the path. We can no longer follow in the footprints of previous researchers, whose work in creating financial models like DuPont and EVA has greatly increased our understanding of the importance of supply chain operations to a company's overall performance. It is time to step off the beaten track to see where our current level of knowledge might eventually lead us.

To help us, we can call on the models we have examined to far, which present information at a level of aggregation that the supply manager can handle, although they certainly require an additional level of desegregation to make them useful at the levels in an organization where decisions are typically based on more operational information. Nevertheless, the supply chain manager can use the elements at the borders of the DuPont and EVA models as interfaces that enable a more detailed breakdown of the metrics into practical, actionable items. Using the information from these interfaces, supply chain managers can organize action items for the resources that fall under their control.

This task will be much simpler if supply chain mangers have some practical guidance on how to build a model that decomposes the most relevant value models – DuPont and EVA – into operational action items that they can implement. This is what I shall now attempt to define.

The Seeds of a New Model

An important part of the supply chain manager's role is to act as an intermediary between the higher-level decision-makers and the hierarchically lower, operational level where the company's resources carry out the strategies decided by the board. The role of supply chain management in the broader matrix of a company's decision-making process is illustrated in Figure 7.1.

The figure shows that at the higher level – the 'decision view' – the decision-makers need aggregated corporate values that measure ROI, given that make/buy decisions are made at this level. Business impact is another key element at this level, going hand-in-hand with information and visibility on price/performance and risk/opportunity ratios. All the data needed for decision-making at this level are highly aggregated and directly linked with basic raw data that surface from both operations and specific transactions. These regulate the minute-by-minute decisions that govern activities at the lowest level – 'operational view'.

Decision View

- ROI
- Business impact
- Price/performance
- Risk/opportunity

SC Manager View

- Costs/budget
- Schedule/effort/delay
- Utilization and loading
- Resource availability ...

Operational View

- Process/activities
- Product/specs
- Policy/procedures
- Constraints/guides ...

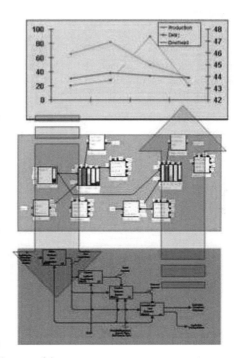

Figure 7.1   The economy of decision-making

At this level we are looking specifically in terms of processes and activities which require sufficient visibility of the delivered products and the specifications for their manufacture. There are some constraints on available resources, which are represented by company policies and procedures of which the decision-makers at this level must be made aware. We can see quite plainly that there is a wide gap, both in terms of the level of detail – which is now more specific instead of highly aggregated – and in the ability to link such distant levels of resources that must ultimately work for the same company with the objective of making it more successful and profitable.

A 'facilitator' is needed to bridge both sides by translating high-level directives, such as increasing ROI by 5 per cent, into operational indications, such as studying and engineering a leaner changeover time for a specific highly expensive asset in order to reduce non-value-added activities in favour of more profitable operations. The ability to break down high-level financial indicators and transform them into their constituent cost elements provides invaluable support to operators at the lowest level, who make their decisions according to extremely detailed and specific guidelines and workflows.

The opposite is also true. It is up to the supply chain manager to aggregate and articulate – in a value-based fashion – all the activities that make up the company's daily operations. The ability to capture the essence of the value generated from activities at the shop-floor level – such as reducing throughput time – and translate it into an indicator that is relevant to the finance team – such as a review of prices due to improved delivery performance – is among the skills now required by a supply chain manager.

Both finance and supply chain managements take a holistic view of the organization. In finance, any transaction that implies the use of corporate resources – including procurement, production, distribution, service and customer engagement – results in events and, therefore, data that end up in the hands of the finance team, although it cannot oversee the specific transactions. Similarly, supply chain managers cannot operate in isolation because the operations for which they are responsible – the processes of planning, sourcing, making, delivering and returning products – run across the entire company. The merest oversight can result in a missed delivery, production stoppages or an incorrect and inefficient distribution of resources, any of which will have a bearing the company's overall results.

Building on Consensus

The model I am about to describe is based on many research findings in the areas of financial supply chain and supply chain performance management. Many of its indications and conclusions have also been heavily influenced by the collaborative efforts of members of the Supply Chain Council, who have demonstrated the importance they attach to this research by dedicating their time to conference calls and offline topics for elaboration, as they are keen to help generate a new reference model for supply chain performance evaluation. All those who backed the research felt that it was extremely important to create a model that would serve as a reference point for their first attempts to close the gap between supply chain performance management and financial value performance assessment.

The SCOR™ model, which every member of the Council acknowledges as the principal reference for supply chain process modelling and performance management, falls short when it has to link operational metrics – those contained in SCOR™ Level 1 and Level 2 metrics – with financial indicators such as the elements of the balance sheet and income statement. Previous attempts have been made to map SCOR™ metrics with financial indicators, but none of these has ever gone beyond very generic and approximate tabulations. However, the research that was performed, and its validation by the team members, highlighted the need for further development of a model that would serve both purposes of the supply chain manager: to link from top to bottom the decision and operational views (see Figure 7.1) by breaking down high-level, aggregated financial performance indicators into operational key drivers; and to link from bottom to top, aiming to provide the necessary support to an organization's operational levels which want to communicate the value of their activities in a more value-oriented fashion to the company's decision-makers and, therefore, to the market as a whole.

Building a New Model

To be successful, a new model must work in both directions. First, it must link expected financial performance results to the actionable practices of supply chain management that will most likely lead to an improvement in those results – the top-to-bottom path illustrated in Table 7.1. The user of the model will then be able to assess the company's current status in terms of financially-related results – delving into the language of the executives at the 'decision view' level

Table 7.1   Steps in building the top-to-bottom model

Step	Description
1	Identify and select elements of financial performance.
2	Identify and select supply chain practices.
3	Map elements of financial performance with the supply chain practices.
4	Build a dashboard of financial performance indicators. Ensure that these indicators are tightly connected to supply chain management performance.
5	Quantify the value of the indicators of step 4 with current company data.
6	Establish a set of benchmark reference data (for example, competitors, industry sector average, internal business units).
7	Compare the company data with the benchmark.
8	Determine the major performance gaps.
9	Identify the supply chain practices that contribute to closing the gaps.
10	Examine the results of the model. These practices are the ones that the supply chain manager will recommend to the supply chain team with the objective of closing the gaps of the company's financial performance.

– and then convert the improvement actions into operational practices that are more easily carried out by the resources at the 'operational view' level. Second, the model has to support the supply chain manager in translating the language of supply chain management performance into strategic business objectives that belong at the 'decision view' level – the bottom-to-top path. This requires an evaluation of the consequences of decisions taken in order to tailor the supply chain to the needs of the market, which must be represented in terms of high-level performance metrics, and must show how they affect the way in which a business is managed.

Furthermore, any new model must provide a user-friendly interface so that the user can fully exploit the results and respond to them with immediate action. Currently, the dashboard view is considered to be the most accessible way of transforming information into actionable items, so the model must fit with this kind of interface.

The individual steps listed in Table 7.1 are examined in more detail below, in order to define the financial and operational indicators that apply to each one, and to interpret them in a way that will lead us always to the next step.

STEP 1: IDENTIFY AND SELECT ELEMENTS OF FINANCIAL PERFORMANCE

There are many indicators that measure financial performance. Typically these are called financial 'ratios' because they express financial performance as a ratio between factors rather than as a pure number. Some examples of frequently used financial ratios are:

- inventory turnover (COGS/average inventory)

- total asset turnover (sales/total assets)

- average collection period (accounts receivable/credit sales per day)

- asset turnover (sales/average total assets)

- return on assets (ROA) (profit after taxes/average total assets)

- earnings per share (net income/weighted average number of common shares outstanding)

- current ratio (current assets/current liabilities) – a measure of a company's liquidity. A current ratio of 1.5 or greater is usually sufficient to meet short-term needs

- quick ratio ((current assets – inventories) ÷ current liabilities) – a measure of how easily a company can pay its debts without selling inventory. This is the same as the current ratio except that it takes inventories out of the equation. A quick ratio above 1.0 generally indicates that the company can meet its obligations

- working capital (current assets – current liabilities) – a measure of a company's ability to pay short-term obligations for working capital.

To keep things simple, despite the fact that we are dealing with complex matters, I have chosen the elements of the balance sheet and income statement that most closely relate to supply chain management activities. These are not only easy to read – even for those who are not financial experts and have had only limited training – but are also readily accessible in financial magazines and on corporate websites, especially for publicly traded companies.

The decision to use the basic elements of financial reports certainly simplifies the process of retrieving the basic source data, but it does not eliminate the need to select them very carefully in order to ensure that we use the right ones for our analysis. Some balance sheets and income statements seem quite complex and highly detailed as illustrated by Figures 7.2 and 7.3, which show a balance sheet and an income statement respectively.

The elements I finally selected and which I recommend are the following.

From the balance sheet (see Figure 7.2)

- *Inventories*   This element is relevant from both a financial and a supply chain perspective, as it represents the amount of cash tied up in physical goods but not yet transformed and sold to the market, or utilized to generate free cash. The role of finance is to reduce the cost of the immobilized cash by negotiating better values for cost of capital. The supply chain must apply its best practices to reduce the volume of goods to only the level required to ensure constant deliveries to the customers and the necessary level of flexibility to respond to unexpected fluctuations in demand and supply from customers and suppliers.

- *Accounts receivable*   Financially, this represents the amount of money owed that is still in the hands of customers. It is considered as a company asset because it is due to arrive and can be used as real cash in many transactions. Invoice factoring, for example, is a form of corporate finance whereby a business sells its accounts receivable – in the form of invoices – at a discount. When the debts are sold without recourse, the business is no longer dependent on the conversion of accounts receivable to cash from the actual payments from their customers. Businesses benefit from invoice factoring in that they accelerate cash flow by obtaining money from the factor equal to the face value of the sold accounts receivable, less a factor's fee. From its point of view, the supply chain must ensure the timely delivery of goods in the right quantities, in the right quality, at the right time.

BALANCE SHEET

Total net sales and revenue	193,517
Cost of sales and other expenses (COGS)	159,951
Selling, general and administrative expenses (SG&A)	20,394
Interest expense	11,980
Total costs and expenses	192,325
Income from continuing operations before income taxes, equity income and minority interests	1,192
Income tax (benefit) expense	(911)
Equity income and minority interests	702
Income from continuing operations	2,805
(Loss) from discounted operations	–
Gain on sale of discounted operations	–
Net income	2,805

Figure 7.2   A balance sheet

ASSETS

Cash and cash equivalents	35,993
Other marketable securities	**21,737**
Total cash and marketable securities	57,730
Finance receivables – net	199,600
Loans held for sale	19,934
Accounts and notes receivable (less allowances)	21,236
Inventories (less allowances)	12,247
Deferred income taxes	26,241
Net equipment on operating leases (less accumulated depreciation)	34,214
Equity in net assets of nonconsolidated affiliates	6,776
Property – net	39,020
Intangible assets – net	4,925
Other assets	57,680
Total assets	**479,603**

LIABILITIES AND STOCKHOLDERS' EQUITY

Accounts payable (principally trade)	28,830
Notes and loans payable	300,279
Post-retirement benefits other than pensions	28,111
Pensions	9,455
Deferred income taxes	7,078
Accrued expenses and other liabilities	77,727
Total liabilities	451,480
Minority interests	397
Stockholders' equity	942
Capital surplus (principally additional paid-in capital)	15,241
Retained earnings	14,428
Subtotal	30,611
Accumulated foreign currency translation adjustments	(1,194)
Net unrealized gains on derivatives	589
Net unrealized gains on securities	751
Minimum pension liability adjustment	(3,031)
Accumulated other comprehensive loss	(2,885)
Total stockholders' equity	27,726
Total liabilities and stockholders' equity	**479,603**

Figure 7.3   An income statement

- *Cash* This indicates the most liquid form of assets, which have a fixed value and can be easily converted to currency. Available cash is the measure of the finance department's ability to provide the company with the necessary monetary resources to make new investments and fund new initiatives. As for physical goods, any excess cash can be considered as a waste. Available cash not reinvested in company initiatives or activities is of little value. The role of supply chain managers is to ensure the most profitable use of the available cash by reducing waste in the operations under their responsibility.

- *Property, plant and equipment* From a financial perspective this component represents the available physical assets with which a company can generate and sell the products or services its customers requires. Any redundancy – if not properly planned and foreseen – immediately adds to the financial burden through depreciation. This process of cost allocation is the recognition that a portion of the asset's cost – the part that will never be recovered through resale or disposal of the asset – was used up in the generation of revenues for that time period. The supply chain, therefore, is responsible for making the best use of these assets as part of its balancing act with the organization's overall profitability. Merely using the equipment or plant capacity just to keep the machine running is of no value until the goods produced are effectively sold to the market.

- *Accounts payable* The cash held by the company before it is used to pay suppliers. This is a form of liability that denotes the amount the company is charged as a result of the goods and services it has bought and used. The objective of finance is to keep this money in the company's hands as long as possible. The role of the supply chain is to provide suppliers with improved visibility and more reliable information, so that the value of the service and information provided is 'paid' by the suppliers in terms of allowing extended payment terms.

From the income statement (see Figure 7.3)

- *Sales* This is the top-line indicator on the income statement and essential for any model. The role of supply chain management here is to ensure proper and profitable delivery of all the goods and services that contribute to this metric.

- *Sales returns and allowances*   Another top-line figure, this indicator is seen by the finance team as a value that reduces the amount of sales. From a supply chain perspective it quantifies the inefficiencies that exist in supply chain operations. This figure is missing from Figure 7.3 as it has been netted off against sales.

- *Cost of goods sold*   COGS is the principal element that reduces the income from sales and must therefore be kept under careful control to ensure that the company continues to run profitably. Finance focuses on identifying all the possible sources of cost, while the supply chain must work in concert with the purchasing department to identify opportunities for reducing the cost of purchased goods and services.

- *Selling, general and administrative*   SG&A are seen by finance as 'indirect' costs, insofar as they represent the expenses incurred in managing a business – employee salaries, legal and professional fees, utilities, insurance, depreciation of office building and equipment, stationery and supplies. The role of the supply chain is to minimize these hidden costs, which can be incurred through working manually instead of using automated systems or through sharing plans with customers and suppliers using old-fashioned fax technology that requires manual intervention and is subject to errors, rather than adopting more collaborative and integrated e-commerce and e-business applications.

STEP 2: IDENTIFY AND SELECT SUPPLY CHAIN PRACTICES

Most supply chain management practices must be general in their nature and widely acknowledged, though there is room to add industry-specific practices where appropriate. To be applicable to any industry, the model we are constructing must be formulated at the general level, although the framework it provides will enable specific practices to inform its future development.

The initial set of practices I have selected is represented by the SCOR™ model's list of best practices. According to the SCOR™ model, a practice is a 'current, structured, proven and repeatable method for making a positive impact on desired operational results'. The practices show operational improvement related to the stated goals and could be linked to key metrics. The impact should show either as gain in speed, revenues or quality or as a reduction in resource utilization, costs, losses or returns.

The SCOR™ model lists, in its appendix, more than 430 practices. Some of them can be seen in Figure 7.4.

The large number of best practices listed in the SCOR™ model is not a cause for concern about complexity. What matters is not the quantity of practices, but to highlight those practices that can have a strong and significant impact on the major financial indicators established in Step 1. It is worth reminding ourselves that the practices of the model derive from real cases where practitioners have adopted them to solve specific performance problems in their supply chains.

BEST PRACTICE	DEFINITION	PROCESS
Demand-Pull Manufacturing, Including Active Reduction of Manufacturing Systems Time and WIP Through the Use of Demand-Pull Mechanisms and Visual Controls	Support of demand-pull mechanisms (Kanban, replenishment signals, etc.) based on rate schedules and user-defined minimum/maximum trigger points	M1.1 Schedule Production Activities M3 Engineer-to-Order M1 Make-to-Stock M2.1 Schedule Production Activities
Demand-Pull Mechanisms; Kanban Replenishment Signals from Stockroom, Intermediate Products, or Subassembly Area	None identified	M1.2 Issue Product M1.2 Issue Material M2.2 Issue Sourced/In-Process Product M3.3 Issue Sourced/In-Process Product
Design For Production	Table of manufacturing capacities or design envelops (capacities; envelop sizes; tank, vessel or batch sizes)	EM.1 Manage Production Rules
Design/Upgrade Production Equipment to Maximize Flexibility and Avoid Line Stoppages	Machine productivity and downtime monitoring	M3.4 Produce and Test
Develop and Clarify Mutually Understood Cycle Times to Process Return Authorizations	Clarification as to who will pay in-bound and out-bound freight cost	SR1.3 Request Defective Return Authorization SR3.3 Request Excess Return Authorization
Develop Local Receiving Process Close to Repair	Minimize time spent in product movement	DR3.3 Receive Excess Product DR1.3 Receive Defective Product DR2.3 Receive MRO Product
Develop Proactive Transit Damage Programs	None Identified	ER.6 Manage Return Transportation

Figure 7.4   SCOR™ model best practices

STEP 3: MAP ELEMENTS OF FINANCIAL PERFORMANCE WITH THE SUPPLY CHAIN PRACTICES

The next stage requires the creation of a mapping table to connect financial indicators with operational activities and practices. In fact, the most natural way to ensure that financial results are achieved through the execution of specific operational activities is to first assess what those activities are and then to correlate them with the targeted financial results. The mapping table, therefore, reflects the correlations between supply chain management performance indicators and financial results.

There are two ways in which we can build the correlation table between financial performance and supply chain management actions. The most precise method is to use a table of statistical correlations. The problem with this is that numerous data points are required in order to increase the accuracy of statistical elaboration because there are no common metrics – or at least very few – that measure supply chain performance. The abundant financial performance data of large and small companies cannot therefore be merely correlated with the metrics of supply chain performance, simply because these are not measured the same way and are not publicly available for batch statistical calculation. Consequently, the Supply Chain Council currently recommends the use of a common set of performance metrics for supply chain management operations.

The fact that there are presently no databases that collect standard and generally recognized supply chain performance metrics and relate them to financial results does not necessarily mean, however, that there are no statistically quantifiable correlations.

That connection – supply chain excellence directly linked to financial performance – is a key. However, the commonly accepted reference supply chain metrics are limited and the number of possible actions available to the supply chain manager is therefore small. If we look for statistics to build the correlations, the only metrics that can be used for any company we want to assess are:

- inventory turns

- cost of goods sold as a percentage of revenue

- return on assets.

This confirms the recurring problem mentioned above: the commonly accepted reference supply chain metrics are limited and the number of possible actions available to the supply chain manager to improve such metrics is therefore small. Yet a metric must be used to identify, select and execute the practices that will most likely close the gap between the current and desired future state.

Another option is to build a mapping table based on peer review and consensus. This means working in a team to agree on all the aspects of the correlations. The most important factors here are mutual respect and a shared objective. Involving practitioners with different expertises allows the team to evaluate all aspects of each connection between financial results and supply chain performance. Any assumed caveats are immediately brought to light, and a common consensus can be established as to which assumptions can be accepted and to what extent they can be incorporated into the final analysis.

Each participant has offline homework to do before reporting to the group in monthly – sometimes weekly – conference calls, in which they attempt to validate the results of the team member's work and decide on the next immediate course of action. I feel that this approach works well because it captures the experiences and the needs of each practitioner and is based on commonly accepted assumptions and groundwork rather than on elegant mathematical formulae with poor substance. Statistical results would certainly help on a more quantitative level and would be less prone to subjective opinion and therefore less open to debate. However, given the problems with the quality of data sources mentioned previously, the effort required to collect such data is prohibitive and, judging from the feedback I have received from end-users, worthless. Supply chain and financial managers do not seem ready to acknowledge the value and credibility of statistically elaborated correlations between·financial results and supply chain operations. I believe they would have too many questions about how the data are calculated, their sources and the assumptions behind the numbers, and, consequently, they would find it hard to accept the results as valuable reference benchmarks for assessing their company's performance.

I feel it is important to make this point in order to explain why the guidelines for constructing the model I will go on to propose are derived from personal research and validated through a consensus-based approach. The proposed model is simple and also devoid of any statistical support, yet it offers an important starting-point for all those supply chain managers who are eager to elevate their role within their companies. It also provides a new way of approaching the issue of how to communicate the true value of the supply chain.

Experience and peer consensus have identified the following as the most appropriate way of approaching the task of Step 3 in building the top-to-bottom model. The mapping must proceed in sequence, best practice after best practice, with a one-to-one evaluation and assessment of the impact on balance sheet and income statement indicators. Figure 7.5 shows a short extract from the model, which gives us a better illustration of this very important step.

Available-to-promise (ATP)   We need to follow the example line-by-line in order to appreciate how the mapping is constructed. The first – and widely used – practice in the example is available-to-promise (ATP) which enables supply chain managers to provide immediate feedback to customer requests regarding the possibility of receiving specific products or services in the expected quantity and at a specified date. The mapping serves to evaluate which income statement and balance sheet figures are affected by the execution of this practice.

Let us look at the assessed mappings and explain them individually, in order to appreciate the importance of this step in the construction of the final top-to-bottom model, also known as the EVA model.

Sales   ATP impacts on sales because an increased ability to provide an immediate response to customer requests regarding the availability to deliver in the right quantity and at the right time certainly provides an opportunity to sell more units. At the same time, existing customers are encouraged to do business with the company because of its improved level of credibility and trustworthiness. Well-practised ATP not only increases a company's chances of acquiring new customers, but also helps it retain existing ones. The overall result is an increase in sales.

Sales returns and allowances   This figure makes a negative contribution to the positive results of sales. However, if the organization can provide better information on the likelihood that it can meet its customers' requests, it is likely that customer orders will subsequently be fulfilled according to expectations. Companies must avoid delivering the wrong items, wrong quantities and wrong specifications, as doing so will decrease the number of returns from unsatisfied customers and reduce the financial impact of sales returns. The company sales department will be also able to communicate more reliable

BEST PRACTICE	DEFINITION	INCOME STATEMENT				BALANCE SHEET				
		Sales	- Sales Returns and Allowances	Cost Of Goods Sold (COGS)	Selling, General & Administrative Expenses	Inventories	Accounts receivable	Cash and cash equivalents	Property, plant and equipment	Accounts payable
Available-to-Promise (ATP)	Available-to-Promise (ATP) provides an availability and feasibility check concerning a customer request or a customer order.	X		X	X		X			
Carrier Agreement	Carrier agreements are agreements between a company and its domestic and global carriers (for both, inbound raw materials and outbound finished goods) specifying service levels, payment terms, and other conditions.		X	X	X	X		X		X
Collaborative Planning, Forecasting, Replenishment (CPFR)	Collaborative Planning, Forecasting and Replenishment is a concept that allows collaborative processes across the supply chain, using a set of process and technology models.... (From www.cpfr.org/intro.html)	X	X	X	X	X	X	X	X	X

Figure 7.5   An example of mapping in Step 3

information, which will reduce the need to provide discounts or allowances to retain customer loyalty.

Accounts receivable   The combined effect of a higher value of sales and a lower amount of returns and allowances most certainly has a positive impact on accounts receivable. This is the amount that customers owe a business, and it is a straightforward consequence that customer debts will be more easily claimed once the supplier has proven its credibility and its ability to deliver goods of the right quality as requested, at the right time and in the right quantity. Realistically, however, not all customer debts will be collected; businesses typically record an allowance for bad debts that is subtracted from total accounts receivable. As the ATP practice enables the company to extrapolate the entire available inventory in all locations and ensure that goods are delivered according to the specifications of a request, it will be up to the company itself to make sure that the clients served with such an advanced technique are of a superior class. It should not be forgotten that ATP requires significant investments not only in terms of IT systems and applications, but also in terms of a disciplined approach among supply chain managers towards implementing a structured process for servicing customers through the use of reliable and constantly updated information on the status of inventories and resources. The 'special treatment' that ATP represents must initially be dedicated to profitable or strategic customers, in order to attract increased loyalty from those customers whose receivables represent a large portion of the company's overall receivables figure.

   In short, it is most likely that the implementation of the ATP practice will increase satisfaction and loyalty among customers – especially the profitable ones. Some unpaid receivables will still remain, but the majority of the collectables will be paid, which will lead to a reduction in the value of accounts receivable.

Carrier agreements   The Step 3 procedure in Table 7.1 is further crystallized when we examine the mapping of another practice, carrier agreements, with the following financial indicators.

Sales   The definition of the practice states that carrier agreements are agreements between a company and its domestic and global carriers specifying service levels, payment terms and other conditions. In modern dynamic markets it is imperative to service the customer in an ad hoc manner, especially if it is an A-class customer in terms of profitability and strategic importance.

Responsiveness to demand and flexibility are attributes that allow a company to maintain competitive parity. Performing such activities in a profitable way creates competitive advantage.

Current market conditions require a clear selection of customer service strategies to ensure company profitability and financial sustainability. There are various models that refer to customer service strategies, and I consider the one proposed by Cranfield Business School, depicted in Figure 7.6, as the most successful in simplifying an issue that could easily become too complex.

Leaving aside the bottom-left quadrant ('Review'), which a company may well drop unless the items therein play a significant role in the company's product portfolio, carrier agreements are a significant contributor to the 'Cost Reduction' strategy in the upper left quadrant. In fact, a revised deal with key transport service providers requires thorough due diligence and a benchmark analysis against market conditions and competition in order to ensure that the deal is closed in line with a contract that optimizes spend and secures competitive transportation fees. A periodic revised analysis of the demands for low-profit/high-volume stock-keeping units (SKUs) and a deeper analysis of the transportation volumes required to comply with the expected customer service levels allows a company to determine the proper transportation resources it requires and the resulting cost of those services.

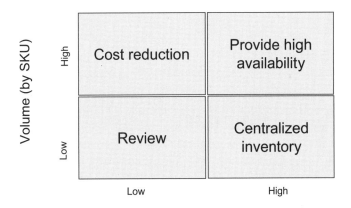

Figure 7.6   Customer service strategies

Source: Martin Christopher, *Logistics and Supply Chain Management: Creating Value – Adding Networks*, London: Financial Times/Prentice Hall, 2005, p. 72.

The 'Centralized inventory' strategy, seen in the bottom-right quadrant of Figure 7.6, serves the purpose of making profit on low-volume items. Furthermore, in this case, the clear and revised agreement with the carrier allows a constant and optimized flow of inbound and outbound materials across the centralized warehouse. Low volumes require a fragmented distribution policy, where the event of less-than-truckload (LTL) is more frequent. Although a comprehensive distribution strategy is necessary to handle the transportation of relatively small freight, a generic transportation contract would acknowledge low fees only in the presence of fully loaded trucks, in order to amortize the use of the carrier's assets.

Less-than-truckload carriers collect freight from various shippers and consolidate that freight in enclosed trailers for line haul to the delivery terminal or to a hub terminal where the freight will be further sorted and consolidated for additional line hauls. Pick-up/delivery drivers usually have set routes that they travel every day or several times in a week, so each has an opportunity to develop a direct rapport with customers. The main advantage to using an LTL carrier is that a shipment may be transported for a fraction of the cost of hiring an entire truck and trailer for an exclusive shipment. Also, a number of additional services are available from LTL carriers, including lift-gate services at pick-up or delivery, residential service at pick-up or delivery, inside delivery, notification prior to delivery and freeze protection. These services are usually billed at a predetermined flat fee or for a weight-based surcharge calculated as a rate per kilogram or ton.

The 'Provide high availability' strategy of the upper-right quadrant relates to products that have high demanded schedules and are more profitable. Here, the company should offer the highest level of service by holding the products as close to the customer as possible and ensuring high availability.

Once again, this strategy can be successfully executed if the firm can call on a strong partner to enable the distribution of high volumes to those customer segments that generate the most profit. This is the case with a full-truckload (FTL) carrier agreement, where the carrier normally delivers a semi-trailer to a shipper who will fill the shipment with freight for a single destination. One advantage FTL carriers have over LTL carriers is that the freight is never handled en route, whereas an LTL shipment will typically be transported on several different trailers.

It becomes clear, therefore, that an organization's ability to seal a contract agreement with one or more strategic carriers by specifying service levels, payment terms and other conditions will give rise to more opportunities to service a larger number of customer segments, which will have an impact on the financial measure of sales.

Cost of goods sold   COGS represents the typical expenses that are incurred by logistics operations:

- cost of manufacture

- raw materials

- transportation costs

- warehousing costs

- lot quantity costs

- information system costs.

A well-structured agreement with one or more key carriers will affect the impact of these expenses by reducing the percentage of the sold goods they represent. As stated in the definition of the carrier agreement practice in Figure 7.5, such agreements can be established as part of a larger initiative to control raw materials and finished goods inventory. These initiatives fall under the heading of third-party logistics (3PL).

3PL can be defined as a supply chain practice in which one or more of a firm's logistics functions are outsourced to a service provider. The kinds of function that are often outsourced include inbound freight, customs and freight consolidation, public warehousing, contract warehousing, order fulfilment, distribution and outbound freight management. Additional value-added services are also available, such as repackaging, assembling and return logistics. The 3PL provider uses its own resources and assets to provide these extra logistics services on behalf of its clients.

3PL providers are used to help a firm stay competitive by keeping it lean, minimizing the assets it must own to run its business and by allowing it to focus on niche areas where it can reduce operational costs. Indeed, it is this last point that confirms the need to map the correlation between the carrier agreement practice and the financial figure of COGS.

Inventories   The impact of implementing the carrier agreement practice on inventories is straightforward, especially when analysed from the upstream perspective – watching the inbound flows of material from suppliers. The ability to optimize management of supplies is foremost on any supply chain manager's agenda. A research study conducted by AMR Research (Figure 7.7) shows that 'supplier failure' is the respondents' greatest concern, and it is placed firmly in the highest category of risk.

Although we cannot question the fact that establishing a vigilant relationship with key suppliers can mitigate potentially negative consequences of supplier disruption, it is equally obvious that supply chain management can help create a safer relationship with service providers by formalizing partnership agreements with carriers.

One of the supply chain techniques that can be adopted to control and assist supplier deliveries is the so-called 'milk run'. In essence, the milk run is a logistics technique for the collection and transportation of goods from suppliers with a defined delivery route, in which various stops are planned

Risk factors: most potential threat

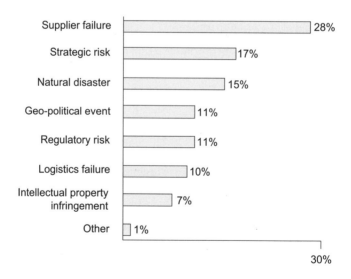

In your opinion, which category of risk poses the most potential threat to your organization?
(n = 89)

Figure 7.7   The supply chain manager's view of threats to business

Source: K. O'Marah, *Supply Chain Globalisation: Risks and Rewards*, London: AMR Research, March 2007.

and executed according to quantities and timing. It can present different levels of complexity, either in terms of consolidated hubs for clusters of suppliers or based on different geographic levels – local, regional, national and international suppliers.

The milk-run technique serves to help foster the synchronized movement of goods into the factory, especially from class B suppliers – those who, in strategic terms, follow behind the class A key partners with whom the firm has established strong contract agreements and from which it derives roughly 80 per cent of the purchased value of raw materials and components. For large corporations the number of class B suppliers can amount to several hundred, making it very difficult to control the flows of incoming goods in a point-to-point scenario with little collaboration (see Figure 7.8).

A carefully managed supply chain should move towards the model in Figure 7.9. Here, a pattern of pick-ups and deliveries is established among suppliers that belong to a predetermined compound.

In this case, the contract agreement with the carrier consists of a pick-up and/or delivery route with several stops. Usually, it will refer to a regularly run route, but it may also refer to a one-time run. The carrier contract will outline

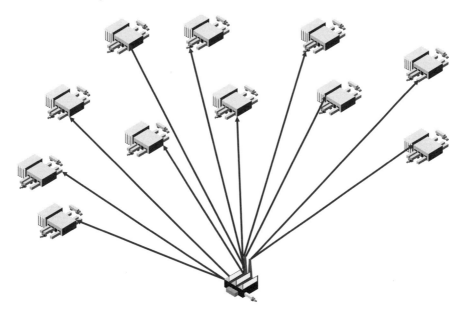

Figure 7.8   Complexity in managing class B suppliers

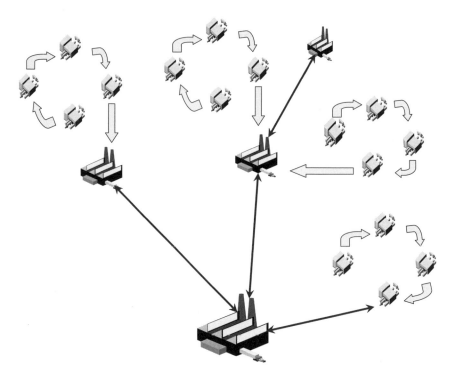

Figure 7.9   Optimizing the management of class B suppliers

the process and services connected to running a route where shipments are delivered and inbound materials picked up in the same run. Inventory levels will consequently be reduced and better controlled.

This validates the mapping of the carrier agreements practice with the inventories element of the balance sheet.

Accounts receivable   The key deliverable for any accounts receivable department is the effective payment of sales invoices. There are many reasons why payment could be delayed, including:

- The sales invoice provided does not include key information required such as purchase order number and goods receipt note (GRN) reference.

- Supporting documentation such as the proof of delivery (POD) is missing or cannot be found, which means that the discrepancy cannot be resolved until it can be seen who has signed for the goods.

- There are differences between the number of goods invoiced and those delivered.

- Invoices are not sent promptly.

- There is no thorough follow-up.

The principal reasons for malfunctions and delays in credit collection clearly stem from a lack of visibility and from passing fiscal and trade documents too frequently across the chain. By establishing a carrier agreement, supply chain managers can positively affect the management of accounts receivable – hence the correlation between the practice and the balance sheet value. The agreement should focus on tying the performance appraisal and the incentives negotiated with the carrier to its ability to positively manage the exchange of documents and information under its control. If this is done, the carrier will actively help its client to avoid the many causes of negative credit collection listed above.

Property plant and equipment   Carrier agreements assume that ownership of the equipment and assets to transport the goods resides with the service provider. Again, the 3PL model contributes to confirming the validity of mapping the practice carrier agreements with the balance sheet of property, plant and equipment (PP&E). In fact, one of the key attributes of a 3PL provider that should be considered a prerequisite is the ownership of the vehicles and equipment needed to transport goods. If the 3PL carrier agreement is expanded to incorporate the management of warehouse and materials handling as well, the savings in terms of reduced equipment and loss of property – by which I mean a reduction in the square metres of real estate that are usually lent or sold to the 3PL – can result in a notably positive impact on the balance sheet.

STEP 4: BUILD A DASHBOARD OF FINANCIAL PERFORMANCE INDICATORS

At this stage it is important to ensure that these indicators are closely connected to the performance of supply chain management. The mapping detailed in Step 3 provides the foundation for those actions that will be executed in relation to the objectives of the company's supply chain. A company establishes the objectives of its supply chain with the aim of improving on its current performance, which must be measured using indicators that capture the quantitative relationships that define the service level provided to business partners, whether they are customers or suppliers.

TIME-BASED PERFORMANCE INDICATORS

As reiterated throughout this book, the time factor provides the best frame of reference by which to qualify and identify the objectives of supply chain performance. I suggest, therefore, that time-based performance indicators should be selected. From the moment it is accepted that the objective of the model is to bridge operational performance with supply chain decisions, it becomes imperative to identify financial indicators that significantly gauge the performance of the supply chain operations and normalize their money value with a timescale factor.

We have already identified the financial indicators in Step 1. Now, we must normalize them according to the time dimension.

Inventories   The time-normalized indicator is days inventory outstanding (DIO), obtained by the formula:

$$DIO = (average\ inventory \div COGS) \times 365$$

This value of DIO quantifies the days of risk-hedging the company has in terms of inventory to offset risks from missed deliveries, unreliable supplies or peaks of unforeseen demand. In very simple terms, the indicator provides the number of days the company could run its operations without acquiring new raw materials or components. In a dynamic and ever-changing market the greater this value, the higher the risk of not having the right material available when needed. In fact, DIO gives a value of how many days the company could theoretically be run using components already in-house. It does not, however, specify if the material is the right one. Since the goods in stock have been purchased according to a forecasted customer demand, a change in that demand profile will most likely mean that some stocked units will be never, or very rarely, used and may ultimately become obsolete, while others will be in great demand and stocks will immediately be depleted.

Accounts receivable   The time-converted indicator is days sales outstanding (DSO):

$$DSO = (average\ receivables \div net\ sales) \times 365$$

Financial managers strive to bring this value as close to zero as possible, as it quantifies the outstanding days between invoicing customers and the collection of funds. This credit is already recognized as a currency value by the market

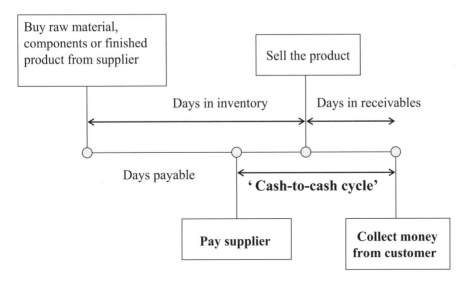

Figure 7.10   DIO, DPO, DSO
Source: D.L. Gardner, *Supply Chain Vector: Methods for Linking Global Business Models with Financial Performance*, Boca Raton, FL: J. Ross Publishing, 2004, p. 170.

since it can be traded as a financial instrument. Financial service providers – such as capital investors – buy and sell these assets with appropriate financial instruments, as we saw when we discussed factoring.

Of course, the money value of a factored receivable offered by a financial service provider comes at a premium. Therefore, even though an unpaid invoice can be treated as hard cash and used accordingly, it is in the company's interest to keep the value of DSO as small as possible.

Accounts payable   The financial reference for the value of the debt owed to suppliers by the firm is translated into a measure of time by the days purchasing outstanding (DPO) indicator:

$$DPO = (AP \div COGS) \times 365$$

While DSO measures the ability of an organization, as a supplier, to manage its relations with the customer base, DPO quantifies the attribute from a buyer's perspective. Company managers, principally the finance director, use this indicator to assess the amount of cash still available before it is used to pay invoices from product and service providers. The overall objective here is to extend payment terms, which will free up cash for investment in other corporate initiatives by keeping it within the company instead of handing it out to suppliers. An increased value for DPO shows that a company has achieved better payment terms.

Cash   The currency value of this financial indicator is converted into the time-based value cash-to-cash cycle time (C2C):

$$C2C = DSO + DIO - DPO$$

Once again, financial managers want this value to be as small as possible. Each extra day means more time when a company's cash is either tied up in uncollected credits, stocked in inventory or withheld. The positive contribution of the withheld cash is factored in the equation with the minus sign before DPO. The greater DPO, the lower C2C, which will improve a company's overall financial status.

Property, plant and equipment   There is little significance in turning the financial indicator PP&E into a time-based equivalent. The proportion of its value from supply chain operations comes from the ability to exploit these fixed company assets. Assets that remain unused for unplanned reasons indicate waste and therefore a greater financial burden. The adjective 'unplanned' is key here. In order to meet changing customer demand organizations must continuously look for ways of maintaining a proper level of agility and flexibility, so that they can balance the spare capacity needed to cope with unexpected peaks in demand with the financial need to pare down all forms of unused production capacity. Return on assets (ROA) is a much better indicator to use, as it quantifies how much profit is generated by one unit of property, plant and equipment asset:

$$ROA = profit\ after\ taxes \div average\ total\ assets$$

Sales   The company's ability to improve this important financial indicator is better expressed along the time axis by using the revenue growth indicator:

$$revenue\ growth = (year\text{-}to\text{-}date\ revenue\ value - past\ year's\ revenue\ value) \div$$
$$(past\ year's\ revenue\ value)$$

Of course, revenue growth does not in itself indicate an improvement in the company's overall performance. Growth must also be viewed in terms of sustainability and profitability if a company is to have the full picture of how well it is performing. However, it is equally important from a supply chain perspective to measure how well operations can support and facilitate growth in sold volumes, in terms of either additional quantities shipped or new channels of delivery.

Sales returns and allowances   The time-related metric for this indicator is again better quantified by comparing current and past values. The objective for a well-managed supply chain is to reduce this ratio to a minimum.

Cost of goods sold   Time-based analysis, as we have seen with other indicators, is of no relevance for COGS. A much better performance indicator is represented by the ratio of COGS on sales, expressed as a percentage:

$$\text{Percentage of COGS on sales} = (\text{value of COGS} \div \text{sales}) \times 100$$

There is a direct correlation between COGS and sales. Other than in the unlikely scenario where sales value grows as a consequence of increased retail price (for example, in a pure monopolistic market), higher quantities sold correspond to higher values of raw materials and components purchased to make these quantities – observed as an increase in the value of COGS.

What really matters is assessing the ability of supply chain operations to maintain a constant balance between the figures for COGS and sales. The objective is to reduce the ratio by lowering the costs incurred in making the final products. This is captured with the percentage of COGS on sales indicator.

Selling, general and administrative   SG&A also better reflects the results of supply chain operations when it is expressed as a percentage of sales. Supply chain practices must strive to do more with less or, more realistically, do more with the same or the same with less. Here, 'more' is defined as an increase in sales. The 'same' would be the current level of staffing and resources, which need to perform more operations – sell more – in the same unit of time because of an increased level of sophistication in the way processes are executed and because leaner procedures have been developed by stripping out non-value-added activities.

STEP 5: QUANTIFY THE VALUE OF THE INDICATORS OF STEP 4 WITH CURRENT COMPANY DATA

The main reason I suggested the indicators outlined above is the fact that they can be immediately calculated simply by looking at the balance sheet and income statements. Their apparent simplicity and their focus on operational decisions are enhanced by the ease with which the basic numbers can be retrieved.

It is not the sophistication of the calculation algorithm that makes a metric more valuable or more significant. Its real value resides in the simplicity with which it can be calculated, the accessibility of relevant data sources, and in its natural correlation with the eventual cascade of corrective actions.

STEP 6: ESTABLISH A SET OF BENCHMARK REFERENCE DATA

Having benchmark data on factors such as competitors, industry sector average and internal business units is very important and needs careful consideration to ensure that the whole concept of benchmarking is properly understood and leveraged.

The general tendency of companies when faced with the need to run a benchmark exercise is to immediately search for external data to quantify the performance of industry peers against predetermined metrics. While there can be little argument against the validity of this approach, I prefer to encourage company executives to seek the data within their own organizations.

I usually encounter two scenarios immediately after companies have completed a benchmarking project, although there is a third that I also frequently observe:

- The gaps between the company values and the benchmark comparison data are too wide.

- The gaps are too small.

- The company does not know what to do with the data it has collected.

The consequence of first scenario is that the executives will start complaining about the quality of the benchmark numbers and the calculation formulae. Alternatively, they may find that the data has been extracted from firms that are not really comparable with their own company. It might also transpire that the circumstances under which the company operates are peculiar and difficult to replicate, although companies may often feel they are different and unique when in fact they are not, or that the assumptions used to calculate the benchmark results are not appropriate. There is also the unwelcome risk for supply chain managers that the comparison is deemed valid and trustworthy, in which case they find themselves on the wrong end of harsh criticism because the company seems to be performing so poorly against its industry peers.

The second scenario tends to lead to an immediate acceptance of the industry data and a general complacency about the results obtained. The consequent risk is that, if the company executives do not have a visionary leader, they will come to believe that there is no urgent need to improve the current status of supply chain operations. The initial momentum that brought the company's best resources to review the current management of supply chain processes, with the aim of investing in initiatives to improve it, could easily dissipate when executives see that the situation is not as bad as they expected.

Both these scenarios can, of course, be resolved if the executives leading the benchmarking project are guided by the vision of those leading the team. While it may be unfair to generalize, I have found that this virtuous combination of skills seems only to reside in a very few organizations I have visited.

To overcome the possible reactions I have just described, I suggest that companies build benchmarks using internal data and then rely on the experience and the best guesses of their managers. For instance, if a firm wants to assess its ability to manage delivery performance, knowing the values of competitors can certainly be illuminating, but if that information is not available then it is not unreasonable to ask the company's sales manager what value he or she thinks would be an appropriate target or benchmark. The real value of this approach is not to get a precise number, but to trigger a collaborative discussion among company executives who, if properly facilitated and moderated, can set a commonly agreed final target value for a particular metric. In doing so, they will have created a benchmark value that overcomes any of the criticism that stems from the first scenario. It also minimizes the risk of doing nothing, which may derive from the second scenario, as there is no debate that an improved target will be foreseen. Moreover, the fact that the benchmark target has been defined through a collaborative effort implies a recognition that some action must be taken.

Taking into account these considerations, I feel that it is advisable to collect data for the benchmarking process through an internal workshop. Of course, additional data from external professional sources, when available, can help better shape the final scorecard, which is what I feel should be the end-result of the process. Figure 7.11 shows an example of such a scorecard.

STEP 7: COMPARE THE COMPANY DATA WITH THE BENCHMARK

The natural next step in our process is to compare the benchmark with company data. This results in a consistent measurement of performance metrics, which allows us to perform an immediate comparative analysis. There are many ways of tabulating the results, but the most effective is to build a radar chart, also known as spider diagram, such as that depicted in Figure 7.12.

It soon becomes clear that the data are immediately comparable, due to the time normalization effect and our decision to calculate the metrics as percentage values. The fact that the indicators are derived from basic income statement and balance sheet data also allows us to estimate the corresponding value that will result from closing the gaps.

DI I	85
DS O	60
DPO	70
C2C	75
ROA	55
Rev Growth	95
S ales Rate/Allow rate	85
% CO GS/Sales	75
% S G&A/S ales	50

Figure 7.11   Benchmark scorecard with relevant indicators

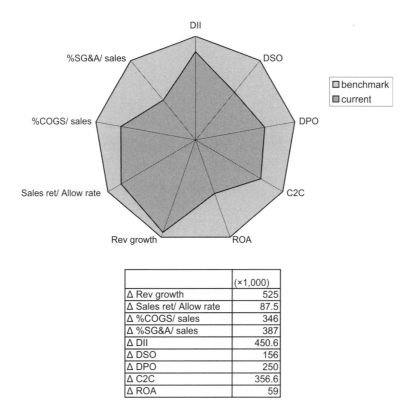

	(×1,000)
Δ Rev growth	525
Δ Sales ret/ Allow rate	87.5
Δ %COGS/ sales	346
Δ %SG&A/ sales	387
Δ DII	450.6
Δ DSO	156
Δ DPO	250
Δ C2C	356.6
Δ ROA	59

Figure 7.12   A radar chart

STEP 8: DETERMINE THE MAJOR PERFORMANCE GAPS

Representing performance metrics in the graphical form of a radar chart makes it possible to identify the gaps between selected benchmarks and current company data. The choice of which drivers to select for further analysis and improvement could be made on the basis of which present a wider gap measured visually by the distance between the internal border – current value – and the external area, which indicates the relevant benchmark. The greater the external area, the more distant the current values are from the desired values.

Of course, it is not only the geometric distance that dictates the prioritization of which gaps to close. The common denominator for such a decision is, once again, the company's strategic objective. A clearly stated objective to improve customer satisfaction and delivery service corresponds to a measured target of a reduced rate of returns and allowances on sales. This means that even a geometrically small gap can imply a significant return in terms of accomplishing the goals of a corporate strategy.

STEP 9: IDENTIFY THE SUPPLY CHAIN PRACTICES THAT CONTRIBUTE TO CLOSING THE GAPS

This last step is the most important, as it provides the set of executable practices that bridge the supply chain with the financial performance targets. This is where the company reaps the benefits from the mapping exercise it performed in Step 3.

If we assume that the gap to close is relative to the rate of sales returns and allowance versus sales, the results of the mapping effort illustrated in Figure 7.5 (p. 186) indicate that available-to-promise (ATP) is one supply chain practice that will close the gap. If, on the other hand, the performance gap to reduce is DSO, then potential improvements in supply chain practices would then be represented by ATP and by carrier agreements. It is worth remembering that DSO is the time-based equivalent calculation of accounts receivable. The practices to select, therefore, are those that map the main indicator of the company's current assets.

STEP 10: EXAMINE THE RESULTS OF THE MODEL

From a conceptual perspective the final outcome of the model will be a dashboard-like chart much like the one depicted in Figure 7.13, with a list of the practices that

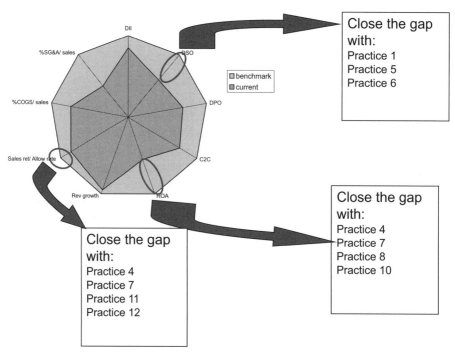

Figure 7.13   The dashboard

supply chain managers will recommend to their teams to achieve the objective of closing the gaps measured in the company's financial performance.

The benchmarked performance indicators show gaps that must be closed. In this example, the gaps to close are relative to DSO, ROA and sales returns and allowance rate. The mappings performed on the correlation factors between financial indicators and operational practices suggest which supply chain practices will have the greatest impact on reducing the distance between the financial indicators.

8

Closing the Gap

In conclusion, I want to reiterate that the constant theme underpinning the creation of supply chain value is strong supply chain management practices that can reduce operating costs and help organizations control their logistics expenses.

It is important to summarize some important factors that lead to such a conclusion. In recent years, when economic circumstances have often been challenging, executives have demanded cost reduction and savings. Supply chain managers have responded by taking the lead in delivering what collectively amounts to billions of dollars of savings in inventories, freight costs, procurement and other costs associated with logistics.

We see a new shift today, in that CEOs no longer view cost reduction as their primary goal. Their focus has moved towards the creation of profitable and sustainable *growth*, using working capital as the key metric.

The research conducted to prepare the material for this book found that many finance executives have still not fully absorbed the intrinsic connection between supply chain competency and corporate performance. This is revealed when finance executives are asked about their involvement with financial supply chain matters. They usually answer that they deploy practices such as: generating working capital in the most efficient ways; finding solutions that optimize cash flow and cash cycle days; optimizing costs, technical resources and implementation efforts; running ongoing treasury administration; focusing on risk in terms of foreign exchange, credit, interest rate, accounting and country risk; and enabling customer–supplier transparency. In addition, they usually declare that they are in the process of considering several products that finance all aspects of the financial supply chain and are looking for products that optimize the financial supply chain process. While these activities are, by themselves, perfectly pertinent, they show signs of a narrow and functional perspective. They do not yet reflect the demands of a more competent and active supply chain. Finance executives are comfortable with a supply chain function that focuses on cutting and controlling costs – one that operationally ensures lean and optimized material flows. Indeed, supply chain management is confused with logistics and materials handling, although, in some cases, it is deemed capable of handling inventory management as well.

My emphasis, however, has been on supply chain management that significantly impacts on corporate performance results. And this happens not by just cutting and controlling costs – a role that, although operationally relevant, is beginning to seem too rigid to modern and forward-thinking supply chain managers – but through developing a competency measured as the ability to identify those practices and activities that deliver positive performance results in terms of value creation. One example of this is improving forecast planning accuracy to reduce uncertainty. When improved forecast accuracy is transferred to supply plans, better terms can be negotiated with key suppliers. Because the suppliers can realize a positive financial return by reducing the safety stocks usually kept to hedge the uncertainty of unreliable forecasts, they can offset an extension of payment terms demanded by the customer. The impact on the accounts payable component of working capital is thus straightforward.

The supply chain manager is also expected to highlight events in the physical supply chain that trigger monetary flows which the financial competence, rigour and skills of the corporate treasurer are able to transform into beneficial inputs to corporate performance. This becomes practically evident as soon as we envision the flows and transactions in the supply chain as a continuous cascade of interconnected working capital cycles. Each stage of the supply network is a supplier of downstream parties and a client of upstream parties. The whole chain is a series of payables, receivables and inventory links. It is the treasurer's role to finance inventory from raw materials through finished goods, and to extend accounts payables through supplier financing. However, it becomes a much more valuable and effective task if it is executed in parallel with the 'owner; of the chain – that is, the supply chain manager.

Closing the Gap by Removing the Barriers

If the supply chain manager is not involved, the finance department will fail to appreciate the true value of investment in the supply chain, and will only sporadically collaborate with supply chain management when a specific problem demands its attention. For that reason, supply chain professionals must be ready to deliver value through their own initiatives in order to support their companies' strategic vision, proving that all successful business strategies have supply chain processes at their core. Nevertheless, supply chain managers need additional support if they are to make a greater contribution to working capital. This support is increasingly likely to come from new entrants into the supply chain arena – namely, banks and financial services providers who are now carving out a whole new domain within the sector of collaborative finance.

Supply chain management has been defined as a disciplined blend of time-based practices and technologies that support users in the design, plan, source, make, deliver, service and return of goods, information and funds relative to products and services delivered to end-users in the global market. Its aim is to carry out such activities in a profitable and sustainable way. This definition emphasizes that flows of money are as important as flows of goods and information, and that careful attention needs to be paid to the impact of supply chain operations and decisions on financial performance. However, there are two kinds of barrier separating the world of the supply chain from the world of finance, and these need to be removed if better results are to be achieved.

THE INTERNAL BARRIER

Investors are now looking at how a company generates value, especially in terms of sustainable and growing profit. Such value is expressed in financial terms. A company's financial representatives speak the language of balance sheet, income statement, cash flows and working capital. Supply chain managers, on the contrary, speak the language of warehouse and inventory management – forecast accuracy, economic order quantity, production planning, sales and operations planning, channel distribution policies and supplier performance evaluation. These 'languages' run in parallel, reciprocally influencing each other, but they suffer from a lack of standards for linking operational and financial metrics. The supply chain manager who is able to prove that the operations under his or her supervision most positively impact on the financial results – and measures the value created in the 'language' of the company shareholders – is well positioned to increase the role of the supply chain function within the organization.

THE EXTERNAL BARRIER

There is also a corresponding 'external' barrier between a company's financial department and the financial services in the market. Supply chains are becoming longer, and more parties are playing a relevant role in their operation: transporters, distribution centres, customs departments, shipping forwarders, free trade zone centres and tax offices. Fragmented point solutions with very limited and poor interorganizational integration and automation with manual processes of dispute resolution, reconciliation and payments are still commonplace. A supply chain will not be truly optimized while electronic ordering takes seconds, goods are delivered the next day, but money is moved after months of reconciliations and clearances.

In today's new supply chain economy, banks are becoming trusted parties that offer cost-effective access to an extensive network and comprehensive service supporting the timely flow of accurate payments between all players in the chain. That means paying attention to the working capital requirements of overseas suppliers, not just the importers. Working capital finance helps smaller exporters buy materials, fabricate their products and ship them to the final customer across a web of intermediaries. When interviewed, banks lament that their corporate counterparts – typically, treasurers and accountants – do not help them gain insight into, and understanding of, the modern relevance of supply chain management practices. To pull down such barriers a new form of collaboration is required. Such collaboration is based on three major foundational elements:

1.   trust

2.   common language

3.   share of value.

Trust requires a genuine confidence that the other party is acting with the purpose of creating a commonly shared win–win proposition. Common language is the channel that drives the efforts and intents of the trusted parties towards a common goal, facilitating communication and the exchange of practices and experiences.

These two elements, however, are necessary, but not sufficient, for a truly collaborative supply chain relationship. In fact, a supply chain is a system of goal-seeking systems, and the optimization of such a system requires negotiation. No-one wants to be the sub-optimized component. It therefore becomes paramount that parties reciprocally agree and acknowledge how to assess and measure the value exchanged.

In summary, the supply chain manager who has learned, and knows how, to transfer his knowledge of the interrelations between supply chain flows (for example, procure-to-pay) with financial flows (for example, invoice-to-settle) to his corporate financial colleagues is well positioned to increase the relevance of the supply chain to corporate value.

Index

Outsourcing IT:
Planning, Contracting, Managing and the Law
Second Edition
Rachel Burnett
978-0-566-08597-0

Constructive Engagement:
Directors and Investors in Action
Nicholas Beale
078 0 566 08711 0

Making Public Private Partnerships Work
Building Relationships and Understanding Cultures
Michael Geddes
978 0 566 08645 X

Sources of Non-Official UK Statistics
Sixth Edition
Compiled by David Mort
978 0 566 08715 4

Buying Knowledge:
Effective Acquisition of External Knowledge
Peter Sammons
978 0 566 08635 2

Go to:
www.gowerpublishing.com/supplychain for
details of these and our wide range of other supply
chain, purchasing and outsourcing titles.

Visit **www.gowerpublishing.com** and

- search the entire catalogue of Gower books in print
- order titles online at 10% discount
- take advantage of special offers
- sign up for our monthly e-mail update service
- download free sample chapters from all recent titles
- download or order our catalogue